MARIJUANA GROWER'S HANDBOOK

THE INDOOR HIGH YIELD GUIDE

by

Ed Rosenthal

Quick American Archives
Oakland, California

Published by Quick American Archives, Oakland, CA

Photographs by Ed Rosenthal unless otherwise identified. Most exposures on Koda-chrome 25 or Ektachrome 400 film. Shot on an Olympus OM2 with Olympus lenses.

Project Manager: Andrew McBeth
Cover: Stefan Gutermuth wgdoublegee
Cover Photograph: Ed Rosenthal
Book Design: Ed Rosenthal and Brian Groppe
Typesetting: Nickel Ads
Illustration: Brian Groppe, Rob M. Harper and Joey Lent
BW Photo Conversion: Sandy Weinstein and Ed Kirwan Graphic Graphic Arts
Color Photo Conversion: Larry Utley Pepper Design
Printed in the U.S.A. by Publishers Express

Library of Congress Cataloging-in-Publication Data
        (Provided by Quality Books, Inc.)

Rosenthal, Ed
        Marijuana growers handbook : the indoor high yield guide/
        by Ed Rosenthal. — 3rd ed.
            p.   cm.
        Includes bibliographical references and index.

        1. Cannabis. 2. Marijuana. I. Title

        SB295.C35R67 1998   633.7'9
                                       QBI97-41428

The material presented in this book is presented as information which should be available to the public. The Publisher does not advocate breaking the law. However, we urge readers to support N.O.R.M.L. and the Marijuana Policy Project in there efforts to secure passage of fair marijuana legislation.

"The wheel is turning and you can't slow down
You can't let go and you can't hold on
You can't go back and you can't stand still
If the thunder don't get you the lightning will . . .
Every time that wheel turns 'round
Bound to cover just a little more ground."

Robert Hunter, The Grateful Dead, Courtesy Robert Hunter

"I never met a drug I didn't like, but I like pot the best."
Tom Forcade

This book is dedicated to Pete Seeger

"God bless the grass that grows through the cracks. . ."

Contents

Preface

In 1969, Richard Nixon initiated Operation Intercept, a program designed to stem the flow of Mexican marijuana into this country. The program forced Mexico to use paraquat on its marijuana fields. In similar actions, pressure was put on Thailand, Colombia, and Jamaica to curtail imports to the U.S.

Domestic smokers became increasingly alarmed at the reports of lung damage after smoking paraquat-sprayed marijuana. In fact, at the time, Dr. Carlton Turner, currently President Reagan's Drug Policy Advisor, developed a kit to determine whether the marijuana a smoker had purchased was contaminated. In addition, infections were reported from smoking imported marijuana which was contaminated by animal feces and mold.

In this climate of health fears and supply shortage, Ed Rosenthal and his colleague Mel Frank wrote **Marijuana Grower's Guide**, which was the most monumentally successful book of its kind ever published. Domestic cultivators took the technology found in **Marijuana Grower's Guide** and developed their own indoor and outdoor plots, no longer willing to rely on foreign supply. The more the government stepped up its eradication attempts aimed at imports, the more mini-gardens and mini-farms began to develop in the U.S. In simple-to-understand language, **Marijuana Grower's Guide** made experts out of gardening hobbyists.

Marijuana cultivation technology has accelerated since **Marijuana Grower's Guide** was written. Advances in lighting technology, hydroponics and propagation left a void of serious literature on the subject. **Marijuana Growers Handbook** is a completely new book which covers all phases of cultivation, including state-of-the-art techniques.

Most experts agree that U.S. growers are the finest in the world. They can get a good yield from the smallest space and have developed hybrids of incredible quality. This indicates that many growers use sophisticated techniques. This book was written to help these people with their gardens, as well as helping novices who are growing for the first time.

IX

The Wall Street Journal recently estimated that there are between 20 and 30 million regular users of marijuana in this country. Other sources put the figure at 50,000,000 users of marijuana in this country. *High Times* calculates that 50% of the marijuana used in this country is domestic. Marijuana will not go away.

Cowardly and reactionary politicians who have maintained prohibition will soon see marijuana legalized. Realistic politicians who see the damage that the marijuana laws have done to the society will change the laws so that they can tax and regulate marijuana. Only homegrowers will be free of the market and government regulation. We are ready for legalization, too. We have the technology for growing superior marijuana and the tools for doing it.

Marijuana prohibition was initiated because of the people who smoked it. The laws continue in effect today for those same reasons. Politicians don't like people who think for themselves, are independent, and who recognize bullshit. They would prefer for each citizen to become a subject, a ward of the state, who is dependent on government for making his/her life decisions. Marijuana tends to let us develop different sets and set perceptions, to see the world a little differently. To change not only what we think but how we think. That's what scares the regulators.

Old man harvesting marijuana plants used for manufacture of hashish.

Women in Madya Pradesh, India stripping buds.

10 acre legal marijuana field in Khandwa, Madya Pradish, India.

Precaution

It is a felony to cultivate marijuana in 49 of the 50 states (it is legal in Alaska). It is legal or tolerated in only a few countries: Holland, India, and Nepal.

Growers use precaution when setting up their gardens. They make sure that their activity arouses no suspicion and that the garden and its contents cannot be seen by unintended observers.

Artificial lighting, usually the main source of light for indoor gardeners, can draw quite a bit of electricity. Electrical systems should be adequate to support the electrical draw. If a large amount of electricity is used, the utility company may investigate the situation for shorts or other drains, including a surreptitious garden.

Growers are circumspect about discussing their gardens. The smartest ones use only the "need to know theory" — that anyone who doesn't need to know doesn't know. Envy, jealousy, and even misplaced morality have made informers of ex-friends.

PART I.

General Information
about Cannabis

Chapter One
Marijuana: The Plant

Cannabis probably evolved in the Himalayan foothills, but its origins are clouded by the plant's early symbiotic relationship with humans. It has been grown for three products-the seeds, which are used as a grainlike food and animal feed and for oil; its fiber, which is used for cloth and rope; and its resin, which is used medically and recreationally since it contains the group of psychoactive substances collectively known as Tetra-hydrocannibinol, usually referred to as THC. Plants grown for seed or fiber are usually referred to as hemp and contain small amounts of THC. Plants grown for THC and for the resin are referred to as marijuana.

Use of cannabis and its products spread quickly throughout the world. Marijuana is now cultivated in climates ranging from the Arctic to the equator. Cannabis has been evolving for hundreds of thousands of generations on its own and through informal breeding programs by farmers. A diverse group of varieties has evolved or been developed as a result of breeders attempts to create a plant that is efficient at producing the desired product, which flourishes under particular environmental conditions.

Cannabis easily escapes from cultivation and goes "wild". For instance, in the American midwest, stands of hemp "weed" remain from the 1940's plantings. These plants adapt on a population level to the particular environmental conditions that the plants face; the stand's genetic pool, and thus the plants' characteristics, evolve over a number of generations.

Varieties differ in growth characteristics such as height, width, branching traits, leaf size, leaf shape, flowering time, yield, potency, taste, type of high, and aroma. For the most part, potency is a factor of genetics. Some plants have the genetic potential of producing high grade marijuana and others do not. The goal of the cultivator is to allow the high THC plants to reach their full potential.

Marijuana is a fast growing annual plant, although some varieties in some warm areas overwinter. It does best in a well-drained medium, high in fertility. It requires long periods of unobstructed bright light daily. Marijuana is usually dioecious;

plants are either male or female, although some varieties are monoecious — they have male and female flowers on the same plant.

Marijuana's annual cycle begins with germination in the early spring. The plant grows vigorously for several months. The plant begins to flower in the late summer or early fall and sets seed by late fall. The seeds drop as the plant dies as a result of changes in the weather.

Indoors, the grower has complete control of the environment. The cultivator determines when the plants are to be started, when they will flower, whether they are to produce seed and even if they are to bear a second harvest.

Chapter Two
Choosing A Variety

Gardeners can grow a garden with only one or two varieties or a potpourri. Each has its advantages. Commercial growers usually prefer homogeneous gardens because the plants taste the same and mature at the same time. These growers usually choose fast maturing plants so that there is a quick turnaround. Commercial growers often use clones or cuttings from one plant so that the garden is genetically identical; the clones have exactly the same growth habits and potency.

Homegrowers are usually more concerned with quality than with fast maturity. Most often, they grow mixed groups of plants so they have a selection of potency, quality of the high, and taste. Heterogeneous gardens take longer to mature and have a lower yield than homogeneous gardens. They take more care too, because the plants grow at different rates, have different shapes and require varying amounts of space. The plants require individual care.

Marijuana grown in the United States is usually one of two main types: indica or sativa. Indica plants originated in the Hindu-Kush valleys in central Asia, which is located between the 25-35 latitudes. The weather there is changeable. One year there may be drought, the next it might be cloudy, wet, rainy or sunny. For the population to survive, the plant group needs to have individuals which survive and thrive under different conditions. Thus, in any season, no matter what the weather, some plants will do well and some will do poorly.

Indica was probably developed by hash users for resin content, not for flower smoking. The resin was removed from the plant. An indication of indica's development is the seeds, which remain enclosed and stick to the resin. Since they are very hard to disconnect from the plant, they require human help. Wild plants readily drop seeds once they mature.

Plants from the same line from equatorial areas are usually fairly uniform. These include Colombians and central Africans. Plants from higher latitudes of the same line sometimes have very different characteristics. These include Southern Africans, Northern Mexicans, and indicas. The plants look different from each

Hindu-Kush plant. The branches are short and stay close to the main stem. The center bud is very prominent. The plant uses relatively little space and has a heavy yield. This is a typical indica plant. From MARIJUANA BOTANY © 1981 by R.C. Clarke, published by And/Or Press, Inc.

other and have different maturities and potency. The ratio of THC (the ingredient which is psychoactive) to CBD (its precursor, which often leaves the smoker feeling disoriented, sleepy, drugged or confused) also varies.

High latitude sativas have the same general characteristics as other sativas: conical form, long bladed leaves, wide spacing between branches, and vigorous growth.

Indicas do have some broad general characteristics: they tend to mature early, have compact short branches and wide, short leaves which are dark green, sometimes tinged purple.

Indica buds are usually tight, heavy, wide and thick rather than long. They smell "stinky", "skunky", or "pungent" and their smoke is thick — a small toke can induce coughing. The best indicas have a relaxing "social high" which allow one to sense and feel the environment but do not lead to thinking about or analyzing the experience.

(A) Male and (B) female Mexican plants. The plants have long spreading branches with thin, long buds. The plant uses a large space for a moderate yield. This is typical of a sativa plant. Illustration by P. Elias from MARIJUANA BOTANY © 1981 by R. C. Clarke, published by And/Or Press, Inc.

Cannabis sativa plants are found throughout the world. Potent varieties such as Colombian, Panamanian, Mexican, Nigerian, Congolese, Indian and Thai are found in equatorial zones. These plants require a long time to mature and ordinarily grow in areas where they have a long season. They are usually very potent, containing large quantities of THC and virtually no CBD. They have long, medium-thick buds when they are grown in full equatorial sun, but under artificial light or even under the temperate sun, the buds tend to run (not fill out completely). The buds usually smell sweet or tangy and the smoke is smooth, sometimes deceptively so.

The THC to CBD ratio of sativa plants gets lower as the plants are found further from the equator. Jamaican and Central Mexican varieties are found at the 15–20th latitudes. At the 30th latitude, varieties such as Southern African and Northern Mexican are variable and may contain equal amounts of THC and CBD, giving

CHART 2-1: The Varieties at a Glance

Variety	Maturity	Outdoor Size (in feet) Height	Width	Branching Pattern	Bud Type	Aroma	High	Buds Density of Bud Indoors	Color (flowers)	Comments
Afghani & Kush	mid-Sept.-Oct.	4-8	3-6	squat, compact, short sidebranches, thick webbed leaves	thick, dense, short, rounded	heavy, pungent, skunky-fruity	heavy, tiring, stupefying	rounded, dense	dark green, purple	The standard commercial plant. Quality varies within population.
Colombian	late Nov.-Jan.	7-12	4-7	conical, X-mas tree, long branches at bottom, tapering at the top, thin long leaves	med. thick, 4-8" long, light to medium density	sweet, fruity, light	spacy, thought-provoking, strong	Tends to run long flower stem, sparse flowered	green, some red	Rarely seen commercially. Needs lots of light and warmth to develop thick colas.
Indian (Central)	mid Nov.-mid Dec.	8-12	4-6	long internodes, big leaves, strong firm branches, elongated conical shape	big, thick, 7-12" long; light-wt. flowers on tiny cola branches.	med fruity-skunky	strong, active, social	large fluffy buds	light green, red pistils	Will run without intense light. Susceptible to fusarium wilt.
Jamaican	late Oct.-Dec.	6-10	3-6	conical, but squatter than Col. Med. leaves, medium branching	long thin colas w/buds 1½"-3" long	light, sweet, musky	medium, active, social	thin, long runs under low light	light green	Adaptable, good weather resistance. Susceptible to fusarium wilt.
Mexican (Northern)	Oct.-early Nov.	8-15	4½-9	elongated X-mas tree, long branches, medium-sized leaves	long, thin 12"-24" colas	light, sweet perfume, spicy	weak, slightly heavy, sleepy	long thin mature well	light green, red	Vigorous plants, fast starters. Some cold-resistance.

Mexican (Southern)	Nov.-Dec.	8-14	4½-9	shorter than northern	long thin 12"-18" colas	sweet	comes on quick; intense, soaring	long, thin, may run a little	very light colored, red hairs	Hybridizes well with Afghani.
Moroccan	Aug.-Sept.	4-9	2½-5	some sidebranching, but most effort in tops	thick, rounded, 3"-6" long	med. sweet to skunky	weak, buzzy	thin buds mature easily	dark green	Good breeding material, lots of variation.
Nigerian	mid Nov.-mid Dec.	6-12	4-7	X-mas tree with strong side branches; long, highly serrated fingers	med. thick, dense; runs in low light	dry-sweet, perfume musk	very strong, bell-ringing, paralyzing	thick, med. length, may run; needs lots of light	medium green	Vigorous warm-weather plant. Needs light to mature.
Thai	Dec.-Jan. and continuing	5-9	4-8	asymmetrical, long branches seek open space	dense, under high light runs otherwise	medium, dry-sweet, spicy	strong, druggy, has energy	fluffy, mature sequentially over months	medium green	Many hermaphodites make growing hard. Buds ripen but plant sends out new flowers.
Southern African	Aug.-Oct.	5-9	4-6	elongated conical lower branches angle up sharply; thin-bladed leaves often heavily serrated	med. thick, may be somewhat loose & leafy	heavy sweet to spicy	uplifting, social	thin buds mature easily	light green	Very variable. Good breeding material.

All of the descriptions are tentative guidelines. They are affected by cultivation technique, microenvironmental conditions, variations in climate, nutrients available, latitude and other factors. Often, several distinctive varieties can be found in the same areas. The most common varieties are described.

the smoker a buzzy, confusing high. These plants are used mostly for hybridizing. Plants found above the 30th latitude usually have low levels of THC, with high levels of CBD and are considered hemp.

If indica and sativa varieties are considered opposite ends of a spectrum, most plants fall in between the spectrum. Because of marijuana and hemp's long symbiotic relationship with humans, seeds are constantly procured or traded so that virtually all populations have been mixed with foreign plants at one time or another.

Even in traditional marijuana-growing countries, the marijuana is often the result of several crossed lines. Jamaican ganja, for example, is probably the result of crosses between hemp, which the English cultivated for rope, and Indian ganja, which arrived with the Indian immigrants who came to the country. The term for marijuana in Jamaica is ganja, the same as in India. The traditional Jamaican term for the best weed is Kali, named for the Indian killer goddess.

Chapter Three

Growth and Flowering

The cannabis plant regulates its growth and flowering stages by measuring changes in the number of hours of uninterrupted darkness to determine when to flower. The plant produces a hormone (phytochrome) beginning at germination. When this chemical builds up to a critical level, the plant changes its mode from vegetative growth to flowering. This chemical is destroyed in the presence of even a few moments of light. During the late spring and early summer there are many more hours of light than darkness and the hormone does not build up to a critical level. However, as the days grow shorter and there are longer periods of uninterrupted darkness, the hormone builds to a critical level.

Flowering occurs at different times with different varieties as a result of the adaption of the varieties to the environment. Varieties from the 30th latitude grow in an area with a temperate climate and fairly early fall. These plants usually trigger in July or August and are ready to harvest in September or October. Southern African varieties often flower with as little as 8 or 9 hours of darkness/15 to 16 hours of light. Other 30th latitude varieties including most indicas flower when the darkness cycle lasts a minimum of 9 to 10 hours. Jamaican and some Southeast Asian varieties will trigger at 11 hours of darkness and ripen during September or October.

Equatorial varieties trigger at 12 hours or more of darkness. This means that they will not start flowering before late September or early October and will not mature until late November or early December.

Of course, indoors the plants' growth stage can be regulated with the flick of a switch. Nevertheless, the plants respond to the artificial light cycle in the same way that they do to the natural seasonal cycles.

The potency of the plant is related to its maturity rather than chronological age. Genetically identical 3 month and 6 month-old plants which have mature flowers have the same potency. Starting from seed, a six month old plant flowers slightly faster and fills out more than a 3 month old plant.

This wasteful office space is easily converted to a productive garden area.
Photo by S. Weinstein

Formerly inefficient office space.

Chapter Four
Choosing a Space

Almost any area can be converted to a growing space. Attics, basements, spare rooms, alcoves and even shelves can be used. Metal shacks, garages and greenhouses are ideal areas. All spaces must be located in an area inaccessible to visitors and invisible from the street.

The ideal area is at least 6 feet high, with a minimum of 50 square feet, an area about 7 by 7 feet. (Square footage is computed by multiplying length times width.) A single 1,000 watt metal halide or sodium vapor lamp, the most efficient means of illuminating a garden, covers an area this size.

Gardeners who have smaller spaces, at least one foot wide and several feet long, can use fluorescent tubes, 400 watt metal halides, or sodium vapor lamps.

Gardeners who do not have a space even this large to spare can use smaller areas (See the chapter ''Novel Gardens'').

Usually, large gardens are more efficient than small ones.

The space does not require windows or outside ventilation, but it is easier to set up a space if it has one or the other.

Larger growing areas need adequate ventilation so that heat, oxygen, and moisture levels can be controlled. Greenhouses usually have vents and fans built in. Provisions for ventilation must be made for lamp-lit enclosed areas. Heat and moisture buildup can be extraordinary. During the winter in most areas, the heat is easily dissipated; however, the heat buildup is harder to deal with in hot weather. Adequate ventilation and air coolers are the answer.

Chapter Five
Preparing the Space

The space is the future home and environment of the plants. It should be cleaned of any residue or debris which might house insects, parasites or diseases. If it has been contaminated with plant pests it can be sprayed or wiped down with a 5% bleach solution which kills most organisms. The room must be well-ventilated when this operation is going on. The room will be subject to high humidity so any materials such as clothing which might be damaged by moisture are removed.

Since the plants will be watered, and water may be spilled, the floors and any other areas that may be water damaged should be covered with linoleum or plastic. High grade 6 or 8 mil polyethylene drop cloths or vinyl tarps protect a floor well. The plastic should be sealed with tape so that no water seeps to the floor.

The amount of light delivered to the plant rises dramatically when the space is enclosed by reflective material. Some good reflective materials are flat white paint, aluminum (the dull side so that the light is diffused), white cardboard, plywood painted white, white polyethylene, silvered mylar, gift wrap, white cloth, or silvered plastic such as Astrolon®. Materials can be taped or tacked onto the walls, or hung as curtains. All areas of the space should be covered with reflective material. The walls, ceiling and floors are all capable of reflecting light and should be covered with reflective

Astrolon reflects light well and doesn't crinkle.

material such as aluminum foil. It is easiest to run the material vertically rather than horizontally.

Experienced growers find it convenient to use the wide, heavy-duty aluminum foil or insulating foil (sold in wide rolls) in areas which will not be disturbed and plastic or cloth curtains where the material will be moved.

Windows can be covered with opaque material if a bright light emanating from the window would draw suspicion. If the window does not draw suspicion and allows bright light into the room, it should be covered with a translucent material such as rice paper, lace curtains, or aquarium crystal paint.

Garages, metal buildings, or attics can be converted to lighthouses by replacing the roof with fiberglass greenhouse material such as Filon®. These translucent panels permit almost all the light to pass through but diffuse it so that there is no visible image passing out while there is an even distribution of light coming in. A space with a translucent roof needs no artificial lighting in the summer and only supplemental lighting during the other seasons. Overhead light entering from a skylight or large window is very helpful. Light is utilized best if it is diffused.

Concrete and other cold floors should be covered with insulating material such as foam carpet lining, styrofoam sheeting, wood planks or wooden palettes so that the plant containers and the roots are kept from getting cold.

Well foiled room. It is easiest to hang wall coverings vertically rather than horizontally.

Chapter Six
Plant Size and Spacing

Marijuana varieties differ not only in their growth rate, but also in their potential size. The grower also plays a role in determining the size of the plants because the plants can be induced to flower at any age or size just by regulating the number of hours of uninterrupted darkness that the plants receive.

Growers have different ideas about how much space each plant needs. The closer the plants are spaced, the less room the individual plant has to grow. Some growers use only a few plants in a space, and they grow the plants in large containers. Other growers prefer to fill the space with smaller plants. Either method works, but a garden with smaller plants which fills the space more completely probably yields more in less time. The total vegetative growth in a room containing many small sized plants is greater than a room containing only a few plants. Since each plant is smaller, it needs less time to grow to its desired size. Remember that the gardener is interested in a crop of beautiful buds, not beautiful plants.

The amount of space a plant requires depends on the height the plants are to grow. A plant growing 10 feet high is going to be wider than a 4 foot plant. The width of the plant also depends on cultivation practices. Plants which are pruned grow wider than unpruned plants. The different growth characteristics of the plants also affect the space required by each plant. In 1-or 2-light gardens, where the plants are to grow no higher than 6 feet, plants are given between 1 and 9 square feet of space. In a high greenhouse lit by natural light, where the plants grow 10–12 feet high, the plants may be given as much as 80 to 100 square feet.

PART II.
Getting Started

Plants grown in the ground in a greenhouse.
The plants grew to 20 feet.

These plants were grown in
one and a half gallon containers using a vermiculite-
perlite-styrofoam mix. The
plants were watered from the
top, and then the trays were
filled with water.

Plants were started in 2 quart
bags (to the right) and
transplanted to 3½ gallon
containers.

Chapter Seven
Planting Mixes

One of the first books written on indoor growing suggested that the entire floor of a grow room be filled with soil. This method is effective but unfeasible for most cultivators. Still, the growers have a wide choice of growing mediums and techniques; they may choose between growing in soil or using a hydroponic method.

Most growers prefer to cultivate their plants in containers filled with soil, commercial mixes, or their own recipe of soil, fertilizers, and soil conditioners. These mixes vary quite a bit in their content, nutrient values, texture, pH, and water-holding capacity.

Potting soil is composed of topsoil, which is a natural outdoor composite high in nutrients. It is the top layer of soil, containing large amounts of organic material such as humus and compost as well as minerals and clays. Topsoil is usually lightened up so that it does not pack. This is done using sand, vermiculite, perlite, peat moss and/or gravel.

Potting soil tends to be heavy, smell earthy and have a rich dark color. It can supply most of the nutrients that a plant needs for the first couple of months.

Commercial potting mixes are composites manufactured from ingredients such as bark or wood fiber, composts, or soil conditioners such as vermiculite, perlite and peat moss. They are designed to support growth of houseplants by holding adequate amounts of water and nutrients and releasing them slowly. Potting mixes tend to be low in nutrients and often require fertilization from the outset. Many of them may be considered hydroponic mixes because the nutrients are supplied by the gardener in a water solution on a regular basis.

Texture of the potting mix is the most important consideration for containerized plants. The mixture should drain well and allow air to enter empty spaces so that the roots can breathe oxygen. Mixes which are too fine may become soggy or stick together, preventing the roots from obtaining the required oxygen. A soggy condition also promotes the growth of anaerobic bacteria which release acids that eventually harm the roots.

A moist potting mix with good texture should form a clump if it is squeezed in a fist; then with a slight poke the clod should break up. If the clod stays together, soil conditioners are required to loosen it up. Vermiculite, perlite or pea-sized styrofoam chips will serve the purpose. Some growers prefer to make their own mixes. These can be made from soil, soil conditioners and fertilizers.

Plants grown in soil do not grow as quickly as those in hydroponic mixes. However many growers prefer soil for aesthetic reasons. Good potting mixes can be made from topsoil fairly easily.

Usually it is easier to buy topsoil than to use unpasteurized topsoil which contains weed seeds, insects and disease organisms. Outdoors, these organisms are kept in check, for the most part, by the forces of nature. Bringing them indoors, however, is like bringing them into an incubator, where many of their natural enemies are not around to take care of them. Soil can be sterilized using a 5% bleach solution poured through the medium or by being steamed for 20 minutes. Probably the easiest way to sterilize soil is to use a microwave. It is heated until it is steaming — about 5 minutes for a gallon or more.

Potting soils and potting mixes vary tremendously in composition, pH and fertility. Most mixes contain only small amounts of soil. If a package is marked "potting soil", it is usually made mostly from topsoil.

If the soil clumps up it should be loosened using sand, perlite or styrofoam. One part amendment is used to 2–3 parts soil. Additives listed in Chart 7-2 may also be added. Here is a partial list of soil conditioners:

Foam

Foam rubber can be used in place of styrofoam. Although it holds water trapped between its open cells it also holds air. About 1.5 parts of foam rubber for every part of styrofoam is used. Pea-size pieces or smaller should be used.

Gravel

Gravel is often used as a sole medium in hydroponic systems because it is easy to clean, never wears out, does not "lock up" nutrients, and is inexpensive. It is also a good mix ingredient because it creates large spaces for airpockets and gives the mix weight. Some gravel contains limestone (see "Sand"). This material should not be used.

Lava

Lava is a preferred medium on its own or as a part of a mix. It is porous and holds water both on its surface and in the irregular spaces along its irregular shape. Lava is an ideal medium by itself but is sometimes considered a little too dry. To give it more moisture-holding ability, about one part of wet vermiculite is mixed with 3 to 6 parts lava. The vermiculite will break up and coat the lava, creating a medium with excellent water-holding abilities and plenty of air spaces. If the mix is watered from the top, the vermiculite will wash down eventually, but if it is watered from the bottom it will remain.

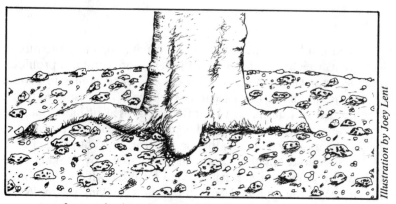

Illustration by Joey Lent

Lava, sand and gravel are all good ingredients in planting mixes.

Perlite

Perlite is an expanded (puffed) volcanic glass. It is lightweight with many peaks and valleys on its surface, where it traps particles of water. However, it does not absorb water into its structure. It does not break down easily and is hard to the touch. Perlite comes in several grades with the coarser grade being better for larger containers. Perlite is very dusty when dry. To eliminate dust, the material is watered to saturation with a watering can or hose before it is removed from the bag. Use of masks and respirators is important.

Rockwool

Rockwool is made from stone which has been heated then extruded into thin strands which are something like glass wool. It absorbs water like a wick. It usually comes in blocks or rolls. It can be used in all systems but is usually used in conjunction with drip emitters. Growers report phenomenal growth rates using rockwool. It is also very convenient to use. The blocks are placed in position or it is rolled out. Then seeds or transplants are placed on the material.

Sand

Sand is a heavy material which is often added to a mixture to increase its weight so that the plant is held more firmly. It promotes drainage and keeps the mix from caking. Sand comes in several grades too, but all of them seem to work well. The best sand to use is composed of quartz. Sand is often composed of limestone; the limestone/sand raises pH, causing micronutrients to precipitate, making them unavailable to the plants. It is best not to use it.

Limestone-containing sand can be "cured" by soaking in a solution of water and superphosphate fertilizer which binds with the surface of the lime molecule in the sand, making the molecule temporarily inert. One pound of superphosphate is used to 5 gallons of water. It dissolves best in hot water. The sand should sit in this for 6–12 hours and then be rinsed. Superphosphate can be purchased at most nurseries.

Horticultural sand is composed of inert materials and needs no curing. Sand must be made free of salt if it came from a salt-water area.

Sphagnum Moss

Sphagnum or peat moss is gathered from bogs in the midwest. It absorbs many times its own weight in water and acts as a buffer for nutrients. Buffers absorb the nutrients and hold large amounts in their chemical structure. The moss releases them gradually as they are used by the plant. If too much nutrient is supplied, the moss will act on it and hold it, preventing toxic buildups in the water solution. Moss tends to be acidic so no more than 20% of the planting mix should be composed of it.

Styrofoam Pellets

Styrofoam is a hydrophobic material (it repels water) and is an excellent soil mix ingredient. It allows air spaces to form in the mix and keeps the materials from clumping, since it does not bond with other materials or with itself. One problem is that it is lighter than water and tends to migrate to the top of the mix. Styrofoam is easily used to adjust the water-holding capacity of a mix. Mixes which are soggy or which hold too much water can be "dried" with the addition of styrofoam. Styrofoam balls or chips no larger than a pea should be used in fine-textured mixtures. Larger styrofoam pieces can be used in coarse mixes.

Vermiculite

Vermiculite is processed puffed mica. It is very lightweight but holds large quantities of water in its structure. Vermiculite is available in several size pieces. The large size seems to permit more aeration. Vermiculite breaks down into smaller particles over a period of time. Vermiculite is sold in several grades based on the size of the particles. The fine grades are best suited to small containers. In large containers, fine particles tend to pack too tightly, not leaving enough space for air. Coarser grades should be used in larger containers. Vermiculite is dusty when dry, so it should be wet down before it is used.

Mediums used in smaller containers should be able to absorb more water than mediums in larger containers. For instance, seedlings started in 1 to 2 inch containers can be planted in plain vermiculite or soil. Containers up to about one gallon can be filled with a vermiculite-perlite or soil-perlite mix. Containers larger than that need a mix modified so that it does not hold as much water and does not become soggy. The addition of sand, gravel, or styrofoam accomplishes this very easily.

Here are lists of different mediums suitable for planting: Below is a list of the moist mixtures, suitable for the wick system, the reservoir system and drip emitters which are covered in Chapter 9.

CHART 7-1-A: MOIST PLANTING MIXES

1) 4 parts topsoil, 1 part vermiculite, 1 part perlite. Moist, contains medium-high amounts of nutrients. Best for wick and hand-watering.

2) 3 parts topsoil, 1 part peat moss, 1 part vermiculite, 1 part perlite, 1 part styrofoam. Moist but airy. Medium nutrients. Best for wick and hand-watering.

3) 3 parts vermiculite, 3 parts perlite, 1 part sand, 2 parts pea-sized gravel. Moist and airy but has some weight. Good for all systems, drains well.

4) 5 parts vermiculite, 5 parts perlite. Standard mix, moist. Excellent for wick and drip emitter systems though it works well for all systems.

5) 3 parts vermiculite, 1 part perlite, 1 part styrofoam. Medium dry mix, excellent for all systems.

6) 2 parts vermiculite, 1 part perlite, 1 part styrofoam, 1 part peat moss. Moist mix.

7) 2 parts vermiculite, 2 parts perlite, 3 parts styrofoam, 1 part sphagnum moss, 1 part compost. Medium moisture, small amounts of slow-releasing nutrients, good for all systems.

8) 2 parts topsoil, 2 parts compost, 1 part sand, 1 part perlite. Medium-moist, high in slow-release of organic nutrients, good for wick and drip systems, as well as hand watering.

9) 2 parts compost, 1 part perlite, 1 part sand, 1 part lava. Drier mix, high in slow-release of nutrients, drains well, good for all systems.

10) 1 part topsoil, 1 part compost, 2 parts sand, 1 part lava. Dry mix, high in nutrients, good for all systems.

11) 3 parts compost, 3 parts sand, 2 parts perlite, 1 part peat moss, 2 parts vermiculite. Moist, mid-range nutrients, good for wick systems.

12) 2 parts compost, 2 parts sand, 1 part styrofoam. Drier, high nutrients, good for all systems.

13) 5 parts lava, 1 part vermiculite. Drier, airy, good for all systems.

Here are some drier mediums suitable for flood systems as well as drip emitters hydroponic systems (covered in Chapter 9).

CHART 7-1-B: FLOOD SYSTEM/DRIP EMITTER MIXES

1) Lava

2) Pea size gravel

3) Sand

4) Mixes of any or all of the above

Manure and other slow-releasing natural fertilizers are often added to the planting mix. With these additives, the grower needs to use fertilizers only supplementally. Some of the organic amendments are listed in the following chart. Organic amendments can be mixed but should not be used in amounts larger than those recommended because too much nutrient can cause toxicity.

This is an "all ingredients" planting mix. The author took all of the medium ingredients he had lying around. These included coarse and medium-grade vermiculite and perlite, lava, sand, compost, top soil and styrofoam pellet chips. Cottonseed meal, blood meal and lime were added to the mix, which was used in 1½ gallon containers with wicks. Occasionally, the containers were also watered from the top.

Some growers add time-release fertilizers to the mix. These are formulated to release nutrients over a specified period of time, usually 3, 4, 6 or 8 months. The actual rate of release is regulated in part by temperature, and since house temperatures are usually higher than outdoor soil temperatures, the fertilizers used indoors release over a shorter period of time than is noted on the label.

Gardeners find that they must supplement the time-release fertilizer formulas with soluble fertilizers during the growing season. Growers can circumvent this problem by using a time-release fertilizer suggested for a longer period of time than the plant cycle. For instance, a 9 month time-release fertilizer can be used in a 6 month garden. Remember that more fertilizer is releasing faster, so that a larger amount of nutrients will be available than was intended. These mixes are used sparingly.

About one tablespoon of dolomite limestone should be added for each gallon of planting mix, or a half cup per cubic foot of mix. This supplies the calcium along with magnesium, both of which the plants require. If dolomite is unavailable, then hydrated lime or any agricultural lime can be used.

CHART 7-2: ORGANIC AMENDMENTS

AMENDMENT	N	P	K	1 Part in X Parts Mix
COW MANURE	1.5	.85	1.75	Excellent conditioner, breaks down over the growing season. 1 part in 10 parts mix.
CHICKEN MANURE	3	1.5	.85	Fast acting. 1 part in 20 parts mix.
BLOOD MEAL	15	1.3	.7	N quickly available. 1 part in 100 parts mix.
DRIED BLOOD	13	3	0	Very soluble. 1 part in 100 parts mix.
WORM CASTINGS	3	1	.5	Releases N gradually. 1 part in 15 parts mix.
GUANO	2-8	2-5	.5-3	Varies a lot, moderately soluble. For guano containing 2% nitrogen, 1 part in 15 parts mix. For 8% nitrogen, 1 part in 40 parts mix.
COTTONSEED MEAL	6	2.5	1.5	Releases N gradually. 1 part in 30 parts mix.
GREENSAND	0	1.5	5	High in micronutrients. Nutrients available over the season. 1 part in 30 parts mix.
FEATHERS	15	?	?	Breaks down slowly. 1 part in 75 parts mix.
HAIR	17	?	?	Breaks down slowly. 1 part in 75 parts mix.
N = Nitrogen • P = Phosphorous • K = Potassium				

Chapter Eight
Hydroponics vs. Soil Gardening

Plants growing in the wild outdoors obtain their nutrients from the breakdown of complex organic chemicals into simpler water-soluble forms. The roots catch the chemicals using a combination of electrical charges and chemical manipulation. The ecosystem is generally self-supporting. For instance, in some tropical areas most of the nutrients are actually held by living plants. As soon as the vegetation dies, bacteria and other microlife feast and render the nutrients water-soluble. They are absorbed into the soil and are almost immediately taken up by higher living plants.

Farmers remove some of the nutrients from the soil when they harvest their crops. In order to replace those nutrients they add fertilizers and other soil additives.

Gardeners growing plants in containers have a closed ecology system. Once the plants use the nutrients in the medium, their growth and health is curtailed until more nutrients become available to them. It is up to the grower to supply the nutrients required by the plants. The addition of organic matter such as compost or manure to the medium allows the plant to obtain nutrients for a while without the use of water-soluble fertilizers. However, once these nutrients are used up, growers usually add water-soluble nutrients when they water. Without realizing it, they are gardening hydroponically. Hydroponics is the art of growing plants, usually without soil, using water-soluble fertilizers as the main or sole source of nutrients. The plants are grown in a non-nutritive medium such as gravel or sand or in lightweight materials such as perlite, vermiculite or styrofoam.

The advantages of a hydroponic system over conventional horticultural methods are numerous: dry spots, root drowning and soggy conditions do not occur. Nutrient and pH problems are largely eliminated since the grower maintains tight control over their concentration; there is little chance of "lockup" which occurs when the nutrients are fixed in the soil and unavailable to the plant; plants can be grown more conveniently in small containers; and owing to the fact that there is no messing around with soil, the whole operation is easier, cleaner, and much less bothersome than when using conventional growing techniques.

Chapter Nine
Hydroponic Systems

PASSIVE HYDROPONIC SYSTEMS

Most hydroponic systems fall into one of two broad categories: passive or active. Passive systems such as reservoir or wick setups depend on the molecular action inherent in the wick or medium to make water available to the plant. Active systems which include the flood, recirculating drip and aerated water systems, use a pump to send nourishment to the plants.

Most commercially made "hobby" hydroponic systems designed for general use are shallow and wide, so that an intensive garden with a variety of plants can be grown. But most marijuana growers prefer to grow each plant in an individual container.

The Wick System

The wick system is inexpensive, easy to set up and easy to maintain. The principle behind this type of passive system is that a length of ⅜ to ⅝ inch thick braided nylon rope, used as a wick, will draw water up to the medium and keep it moist. The container, which can be an ordinary nursery pot, holds a rooting medium and has wicks running along the bottom, drooping through the holes at the bottom, reaching down to the reservoir. Keeping the holes in the container small makes it difficult for roots to penetrate to the reservoir. The amount of water delivered to the medium can be increased by increasing the number, length, or diameter of the wicks in contact with the medium.

A 1 gallon container needs only a single wick, a three gallon container should have two wicks, a five gallon container, three wicks. The wick system is self-regulating; the amount of water delivered depends on the amount lost through evaporation or transpiration.

Illustration by Joey Lent

A simple wick system using a kiddie pool as the reservoir. The unit is easy to water and simple to maintain.

This unit is available commercially. It has a built-in water gauge and generally works well. However, a brick or piece of 4 x 4 placed at the bottom of the outer container prevents vacuum lock. Courtesy *Geotechnology,* Aromas, California.

Each medium has a maximum saturation level. Beyond that point, an increase in the number of wicks will not increase the moisture level. A 1-1-1 combination of vermiculite, perlite, and styrofoam is a convenient medium because the components are lightweight and readily available. Some commercial units are supplied with coarse vermiculite. To increase weight so that the plant will not tip the container over when it gets large, some of the perlite in the recipe can be replaced with sand. The bottom inch or two of the container should be filled only with vermiculite, which is very absorbent, so that the wicks have a good medium for moisture transfer.

Wick systems are easy to construct. The wick should extend 5 inches or more down from the container. Two bricks, blocks of wood, or styrofoam are placed on the bottom of a deep tray (a plastic tray or oil drip pan will do fine.) Then the container is placed on the blocks so that the wicks are touching the bottom of the tray. The tray is filled with a nutrient/water solution. Water is replaced in the tray as it evaporates or is absorbed by the medium through the wick.

A variation of this system can be constructed using an additional outer container rather than a tray. With this method less water is lost due to evaporation.

To make sure that the containers fit together and come apart easily, bricks or wood blocks are placed in the bottom of the outer container. The container is filled with the nutrient/water solution until the water comes to just below the bottom of the inner container.

Automating this system is simple to do. Each of the trays or bottom containers is connected by tubing to a bucket containing a float value such as found in toilets. The valve is adjusted so that it shuts off when the water reaches a height about ½ inch below the bottom of the growing containers. The bucket with the float valve is connected to a large reservoir such as a plastic garbage can or 55 gallon drum. Holes can be drilled in the containers to accomodate the tubing required, or the tubes can be inserted from the top of the containers or trays. The tubes should be secured or weighted down so that they do not slip out and cause floods.

The automated wick system works as a siphon. To get it started, the valve container is primed and raised above the level of the individual trays. Water flows from the valve to the plant trays as a result of gravity. Once the containers have filled and displaced air

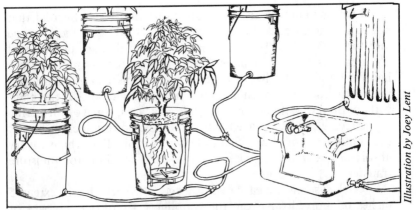

Illustration by Joey Lent

This automated wick system is no longer available commercially, but is not difficult for the home hobbyist to build. The water level is regulated by a float valve. All the containers must be placed on the same level. The float valve is adjusted so only the bottom of the reservoir containers (3-4 inches) are filled.

from the tubes, the water is automatically siphoned and the valve container can be lowered. Each container receives water as it needs it.

A simpler system can be devised using a plastic kiddie pool and some 4 x 4's or a wooden pallet. Wood is placed in the pool so that the pots sit firmly on the board; the pool is then filled with water up to the bottom of the pots. The wicks move the water to the pots.

Wick systems and automated wick systems are available from several manufacturers. Because they require no moving parts, they are generally reliable although much more expensive than homemade ones, which are very simple to make.

Wick system units can be filled with any of the mixes found in Chart 7-1-A.

The Reservoir System

The reservoir system is even less complex than the wick system. For this setup all a grower needs to do is fill the bottom 2 or 3 inches of a 12 inch deep container with a coarse, porous, inert medium such as lava, ceramic beads or chopped unglazed pottery. The remaining portion is filled with one of the mixes containing styrofoam. The container is placed in a tray, and sits directly in a nutrient-water solution 2-3 inches deep. The system is automated

Garden consisting of containers and trays. The trays were 3 inches deep and were filled to the brim. They were watered again when the tray was dry. Bushel containers in the background were filled with soil. Although the soil-filled containers were started two weeks before the hydroponic units, the hydros had a better yield.

A garden in a kiddie pool. The plants are in 3 gallon plastic bags.

by placing the containers in a trough or large tray. Kiddie pools can also be used. The water is not replaced until the holding tray dries.

Passive systems should be watered from the top down once a month so that any buildup of nutrient salts caused by evaporation gets washed back to the bottom.

ACTIVE HYDROPONIC SYSTEMS

Active systems move the water using mechanical devices in order to deliver it to the plants. There are many variations on active systems but most of them fall into one of three categories: flood systems, drip systems or nutrient film systems.

The Flood System

The flood system is the type of unit that most people think of when hydroponics is mentioned. The system usually has a reservoir which periodically empties to flood the container or tub holding the medium. The medium holds enough moisture between irrigations to meet the needs of the plant. Older commercial greenhouses using this method often held long troughs or beds of gravel. Today, flood systems are designed using individual containers. Each container is attached to the reservoir using tubing.

This system utilizes the nutrient film techniques in hydroponics. The triangular tube provides a gentle flow of nutrients along the roots. Courtesy *Homegrown Halide*, Parkland, Washington.

This flood unit sets up easily and supports fast growth. Courtesy *Applied Hydroponics*, San Rafael, California.

A simple flood system can be constructed using a container with a tube attached at the bottom of a plastic container and a jug. The tube should reach down to the jug, which should be placed below the bottom of the growing container. To water, the tube is held above the container so that it doesn't drip. The water is poured from the jug into the container. Next, the tube is placed in the jug and put back into position, below the growing container. The water will drain back into the jug. Of course, not as much will drain back in as was poured out. Some of the water was retained in the growing unit.

Illustration by Rob M. Harper

This manual flood system can be easily made from housewares.

Automating this unit is not difficult. A two-holed stopper is placed in the jug. A tube from the growing unit should reach the bottom of the reservoir container. Another tube should be attached to the other stopper hole and then to a small aquarium-type air pump which is regulated by a timer. When the pump turns on, it pushes air into the jug, forcing the water into the container. When the pump goes off, the water is forced back into the jug by gravity. Several growing units can be hooked up to a large central reservoir and pump to make a larger system. The water loss can automatically be replaced using a float valve, similar to the ones used to regulate water in a toilet. Some growers place a second tube near the top of the container which they use as an overflow drain.

Illustration by Rob M. Harper

A stopper, timer and aquarium pump converts the unit into an automatic system. Several units can be hooked to the same pump.

Another system uses a reservoir above the growing container level. A water timing valve or solenoid valve keeps the water in the reservoir most of the time. When the valve opens, the water fills the growing containers as well as a central chamber which are both at the same height. The growing chambers and the central chamber are attached to each other. The water level is regulated by a float valve and sump pump. When the water level reaches a certain height, near the top of the pots, the sump pump automatically turns on and the water is pumped back up to the reservoir.

One grower used a kiddie pool, timer valve, flower pots, a raised reservoir and sump pump. He placed the containers in the kiddie pool along with the sump pump and a float valve. When the timer valve opened, the water rushed from the tank to the kiddie pool, flooding the containers. The pump turned on when the water was two inches from the top of the containers and emptied the pool. Only when the valve reopened did the plants receive more water.

With this system, growers have a choice of mediums, including sand, gravel, lava, foam or chopped-up rubber. Vermiculite, perlite, and styrofoam are too light to use. The styrofoam and perlite float, and the vermiculite becomes too soggy.

The plants' water needs to increase during the lighted part of the daily cycle, so the best time to water is as the light cycle begins. If the medium does not hold enough moisture between waterings, the frequency of waterings is increased.

There are a number of companies which manufacture flood systems. Most of the commercially made ones work well, but they tend to be on the expensive side. They are convenient though.

The Drip System

Years ago, the most sophisticated commercial greenhouses used drip emitter systems which were considered exotic and sophisticated engineering feats. These days, gardeners can go to any well-equipped nursery and find all of the materials necessary to design and build the most sophisticated drip systems. These units consist of tubing and emitters which regulate the amount of water delivered to each individual container. Several types of systems can be designed using these devices.

The easiest system to make is a non-return drain unit. The plants are watered periodically using a diluted nutrient solution. Excess water drains from the containers and out of the system. This system is only practical when there is a drain in the growing area. If each container has a growing tray to catch excess water and the water control valve is adjusted closely, any excess water can be held in the tray and eventually used by the plant or evaporated. Once a gardener gets the hang of it, matching the amount of water delivered to the amount needed is easy to do.

One grower developed a drip emitter system which re-uses the water by building a wooden frame using 2 x 4's and covering it with corrugated plastic sheeting. She designed it so that there was a slight slope. The containers were placed on the corrugated plastic, so the

Five gallon containers are watered using drip emitters on a timer.

Water drains from the containers, along the troughs formed by the plastic corrugations, into the pump container. The sump pump turns on automatically as the water level rises. The upper reservoir (not shown) is controlled by a closed solenoid valve which is run by timer.

water drained along the corrugations into a rain drainage trough, which drained into a 2 or 3 gallon holding tank. The water was pumped from the holding tank back to the reservoir. The water was released from the reservoir using a timer valve.

Growers make sure to use self-cleaning drip emitters so that they do not clog with salt deposits. About a gallon every six hours during daylight hours is pumped. Drip emitters can be used with semiporous mediums such as ceramic beads, lava, gravel, sand or perlite-vermiculite-styrofoam mixtures.

Aerated Water

The aerated water system is probably the most complex of the hydroponic systems because it allows the least margin for error. It should only be used by growers with previous hydroponic experience. The idea of the system is that the plant can grow in water as long as the roots receive adequate amounts of oxygen. To provide the oxygen, an air pump is used to oxygenate the water through bubbling and also by increasing the circulation of the water so that there is more contact with air. The plants can be grown in individual containers, each with its own bubbler or in a single flooded unit in which containers are placed. One grower used a vinyl-covered tank he constructed. He placed individual containers that

Illustration by Rob M. Harper

This aerated water system was made from a plastic food container.

he made into the tank. His containers were made of heavy-duty
nylon mesh used by beermakers for soaking hops. This did not prevent water from circulating around the roots.

Aerated water systems are easy to build. A small aquarium air
pump supplies all the water that is required. An aerator should be
connected to the end and a clear channel made in the container for
the air. The air channel allows the air to circulate and not disturb
the roots. Gravel, lava, or ceramic is used.

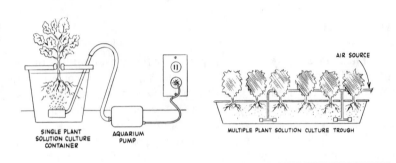

A simple aerated water system.

Nutrient Film Technique

The nutrient film technique is so named because the system
creates a film of water that is constantly moving around the roots.
This technique is used in many commercial greenhouses to cultivate
fast growing vegetables such as lettuce without any medium. The
plants are supported by collars which hold them in place. This
method is unfeasible for marijuana growers. However, it can be
modified a bit to create an easy-to-care-for garden. Nursery sup-
pliers sell water mats, which disperse water from a soaker hose to a
nylon mat. The plants grow in bottomless containers which sit on
the mat. The medium absorbs water directly from the mat. In order
to hold the medium in place, it is placed in a nylon net bag in the
container.

A home-made nutrient flow unit. The water ran along the bottom of the bags constantly.

Individual valves controlled the water flow of each trough.

In this Rockwool system the cubes are placed on a corrugated shelf which is slightly tilted to empty into a trough, which delivers water back to the reservoir. When this picture was taken, the grower was irrigating the plants using a watering can. However, the cultivator eventually automated the system using a drip emitter and a timer.

Chapter Ten
Growing in the Ground

Some growers have the opportunity to grow plants directly in the ground. Many greenhouses are built directly over the earth. Growing directly in the soil has many advantages over container growing. A considerable amount of labor may be eliminated because there is no need to prepare labor-intensive containers with expensive medium. Another advantage is that the plants' needs are met more easily.

Before using any greenhouse soil, it is necessary to test it. The pH and fertility of soils vary so much that there are few generalizations that can be made about them.

The most important quality of any soil is its texture. Soils which drain well usually are composed of particles of varying size. This creates paths for water to flow and also allows air pockets to remain even when the soil is saturated.

Soils composed of very fine particles, such as mucks and clay, do not drain well. Few air particles are trapped in these soils when they are saturated. When this happens, the roots are unable to obtain oxygen and they weaken when they are attacked by anaerobic bacteria. These soils should be adjusted with sand and organic matter which help give the medium some porosity. Materials suitable for this include sand, compost, composted manure, as well as perlite, lava, gravel, sphagnum moss, styrofoam particles and foam particles.

Low lying areas may have a very high water table so that the soils remain saturated most of the time. One way to deal with this problem is to create a series of mounds or raised beds so that the roots are in ground at higher level than the floor level.

Once soil nutrient values are determined, adjustments can be made in the soil's fertility. For marijuana, the soil should test high in total Nitrogen, and the medium should test high in Phosphorous and Potassium. This is covered in subsequent chapters.

Growers use several methods to prepare the soil. Some prefer to till the whole area using either a fork, a roto-tiller or a small tractor and plow. The marijuana plant grows both vertical and horizontal roots. The horizontal roots grow from the surface to a depth of

9–18 inches depending on the soil's moisture. They grow closer to the surface of moist soils. The vertical root can stretch down several feet in search of water. In moist soils, the vertical roots may be short, even stunted.

Soil with loose texture, sandy soils, and soils high in organic matter may have adequate aeration, porosity, and space for roots and may not have to be tilled at all. Most soils should be dug to a depth of 6–9 inches. The tighter the soil's texture, the deeper it should be tilled.

If the soil is compacted, it is dug to a depth of two feet. This can be done by plowing and moving the soil in alternate rows and then plowing the newly uncovered soil. Soil texture adjustors such as gypsum are added to the bottom layer of the soil as well as the top layer, but soil amendments such as fertilizers or compost are added only to the top layer, where most of the plant's roots are. Then the soil is moved back into the troughs and the alternate rows are prepared the same way.

A variation of this technique is the raised bed. First, the whole area is turned, and then aisles are constructed by digging out the pathways and adding the material to the beds. With the addition of organic soil amendments, the total depth of prepared soil may stretch down 18 inches.

Some growers use planting holes rather than tilling the soil. A hole ranging between 1 and 3 feet wide and 1½ and 3 feet deep is dug at each space where there is to be a plant. The digging can be facilitated using a post hole digger, electric shovel, or even a small backhoe or power hole digger. Once the hole is dug the soil is adjusted with amendments or even replaced with a mix.

No matter how the soil is prepared, the groundwater level and the permeability of the lower layers is of upmost importance. Areas with high water tables, or underlying clay or hardpan will not drain well. In either case the garden should be grown in raised beds which allow drainage through the aisles and out of the growing area, rather than relying on downward movement through soil layers.

Soils in used greenhouses may be quite imbalanced even if the plants were growing in containers. The soil may have a buildup of nutrient salts, either from runoff or direct application, and pesticides or herbicides may be present. In soils with high water tables the nutrients and chemicals have nowhere to go, so they dissolve and spread out horizontally as well as vertically, contaminating the soil in surrounding areas.

Plants in ground in greenhouse

Planting holes in basement

Excess salts can be flushed from the soil by flooding the area with water and letting it drain to the water table. In areas with high water tables, flushing is much more difficult. Trenches are dug around the perimeter of the garden which is then flooded with nutrient-free water. As the water drains into the trenches, it is removed with a pump and transported to another location.

Pesticides and herbicides may be much more difficult to remove. Soils contaminated with significant amounts of residues may be unsuitable for use with material to be ingested or inhaled. Instead, the garden should be grown in containers using non-indigenous materials.

Usually plants are sexed before they are planted in the ground. If the soil showed adequate nutrient values no fertilizer or side dressing will be required for several months.

Several growers have used ingenious techniques to provide their gardens with earthy environments. One grower in Oregon chopped through the concrete floor of his garage to make planting holes. The concrete had been poured over sub-soil so he dug out the holes and replaced the sub-soil with a mixture of composted manure, vermiculite, perlite, worm castings, and other organic ingredients. He has been using the holes for several years. After several crops, he redigs the holes and adds new ingredients to the mix.

A grower in Philadelphia lived in a house with a backyard which was cemented over. He constructed a raised bed over the concrete using railroad ties and filled it with a rich topsoil and composted manure mixture, then built his greenhouse over that. The growing bed is about 15 inches deep and the grower reports incredible growth rates.

PART III.
Limiting Factors

There are five factors that can promote or limit plant growth. Each may be a weak link in a chain and the plant can grow no faster than the weakest link allows.

Light, CO_2, temperature, nutrients, and water are all needed by the plant for it to carry on its life processes.

In an indoor environment, it is up to the gardener to make sure that all of these conditions are met adequately so that the plant can grow as quickly and healthily as possible.

This greenhouse required a vertical extension. Even the often overcast light of Amsterdam supported vigorous growth.

Chapter Eleven
Lighting and Lights

Green plants use light for several purposes. The most amazing thing that they do with it is to use the energy contained in light to make sugar from water (H_2O) and carbon dioxide (CO_2). This process is called photosynthesis and it provides the basic building block for most life on Earth. Plants convert the sugars they make into starches and then into complex molecules composed of starches, such as cellulose. Amino acids, the building blocks of all proteins, are formed with the addition of nitrogen atoms.

Plants also use light to regulate their other life processes. As we mentioned earlier, marijuana regulates its flowering based on the number of hours of uninterrupted darkness. (See Chapter 25, Flowering)

Sunlight is seen as white light, but is composed of a broad band of colors which cover the optic spectrum. Plants use red and blue light most efficiently for photosynthesis and to regulate other processes. However, they do use other light colors as well for photosynthesis. In fact, they use every color except green, which they reflect back. (That is why plants appear green; they absorb all the other spectrums except green.) In controlled experiments, plants respond more to the total amount of light received than to the spectrums in which it was delivered.

The best source of light is the sun. It requires no expense, no electricity, and does not draw suspicion. It is brighter than artificial lighting and is self-regulating. Gardeners can use the sun as a primary source of light if they have a large window, skylight, translucent roof, enclosed patio, roof garden, or greenhouse. These gardens may require some supplemental lighting, especially if the light enters from a small area such as a skylight, in order to fill a large area.

It is hard to say just how much supplemental light a garden needs. Bright spaces which are lit from unobstructed overhead light such as a greenhouse or a large southern window need no light during the summer but may need artificial light during the winter to

The floor of this greenhouse is 2 feet underground. It cannot be seen over the backyard fence.

A garden using polished aluminum reflectors which distibute the light more evenly than most reflectors.

Small greenhouse overflowing with pot.

A simple greenhouse constructed from plastic film covering a wooden frame protects the plants from inclement weather and low temperatures.

supplement the weak sunlight or overcast conditions. Spaces receiving indirect sunlight during the summer need some supplemental lighting.

Light requirements vary by variety. During the growth cycle, most varieties will do well with 1000–1500 lumens per square foot although the plants can use more lumens, up to 3000, efficiently. Equatorial varieties may develop long internodes (spaces on the stem between the leaves) when grown under less than bright conditions. During flowering, indica varieties can mature well on 2000 lumens. Equatorial varieties require 2500–5000 lumens. Indica-sativa F_1 (first generation) hybrids usually do well on 2500–3000 lumens.

Some light meters have a foot-candle readout. Thirty-five millimeter cameras that have built-in light meters can also be used. In either case, a sheet of white paper is placed at the point to be measured so it reflects the light most brilliantly. Then the meter is focused entirely on the paper.

The camera is set for ASA 100 film and the shutter is set for ¹⁄₆₀ second. A 50 mm or "normal" lens is used. Using the manual mode, the camera is adjusted to the correct f-stop. The conversion chart, 10–1, shows the amount of light hitting the paper.

Most growers, for one reason or another, are not able to use natural light to grow marijuana. Instead, they use artificial lights to provide the light energy which plants require to photosynthesize, regulate their metabolism, and ultimately to grow. There are a number of sources of artificial lighting. Cultivators rarely use incandescent or quartz halogen lights. They convert only about 10% of the energy they use to light and are considered inefficient.

CHART 10-1: FOOTCANDLES

1/60 Second, ASA 100		1/125 Second ASA 100	
F-Stop	Footcandles	F-Stop	Footcandles
f.4	64	f.4	128
f.5.6	125	f.5.6	250
f.8	250	f.8	500
f.11	500	f.11	1000
f.16	1000	f.16	2000
f.22	2000	f.22	4000

On some cameras it is easier to adjust the shutter speed, keeping the f. stop set at f.4 (at ASA 100):

Shutter Speed	Footcandles
1/60	64
1/125	125
1/250	250
1/500	500
1/1000	1000
1/2000	2000

ENERGY EMISSION IN ARBITRARY COLOR BANDS FOR LAMPS AND TUBES AS STATED PER 100 WATTS ENERGY INPUT

Fluorescent 40 watt standard tubes • 1000 Watt Clear Metal Halide • 1000 Watt MS • 1000 Watt Sodium Vapor

Band in Nanometers	UV -380	Violet 380-430	Blue 430-490	Green 490-560	Yellow 560-590	Orange 590-630	Red 630-700	Far-Red 700-780	Total
Daylight Fluorescent									
Watts	.465	2.97	6.945	5.93	3.147	2.86	1.13	.325	21.982
Percentage	2.15	9.6	27.91	27.38	14.53	13.21	5.22	1.53	100
Cool White									
Watts	.4	1.8	4.95	5.87	4.35	4.22	2.02	.17	23.78
Percentage	1.68	7.57	20.78	24.67	18.27	17.75	8.47	.81	100
Standard Gro-Lux									
Watts	.25	1.75	4.9	2.55	.25	1.1	7.15	.15	18.1
Percentage	1.42	9.67	27.07	14.02	1.42	6.05	39.55	.8	100
Gro-Lux W/S									
Watts	.67	2.67	3.05	3.1	2.07	3.4	4.65	1.72	21.3
Percentage	3.16	12.48	14.29	14.49	9.77	15.93	21.78	8.1	100
Warm White									
Watts	.13	.46	1.15	1.80	2.06	2.13	1.03	.13	8.89
Percentage	1.52	5.15	12.91	20.24	23.17	23.95	11.53	1.53	100
M-1000 Halide Clear									
Watts	33.0	50.0	38.8	60.0	43.8	61.8	21.8	9.8	319.3
Percentage	10.3	15.7	12.1	18.8	14.0	19.3	6.8	3.0	100
M-1000 Coated									
Watts	25.5	50.0	46.8	53.3	42.8	71.5	33.0	14.0	336.9
Percentage	7.6	14.8	13.9	15.8	12.7	21.2	9.8	4.2	100
MS-1000 Halide Clear									
Watts	35.3	54.3	45.0	74.8	44.0	82.3	32.5	20.3	388.5
Percentage	9.1	14.0	11.6	19.3	11.3	21.1	8.4	5.2	100
MS-1000 Coated									
Watts	25.0	6.5	49.5	72.5	45.0	82.0	35.5	19.5	387.0
Percentage	58.0	15.0	12.8	18.7	11.6	21.2	9.2	5.0	100
Sodium Vapor 1000									
Watts	3.5	6	14.8	23	102.3	125.5	35.0	27.5	337.6
Percentage	1.0	1.8	4.4	6.8	30.3	37.2	10.4	8.1	100

Information Courtesy of Christos C. Mpelkas, Sylvania Lighting Products, Danvers, Mass.

"Chart 10-2"

FLUORESCENT TUBES

Growers have used fluorescent tubes to provide light for many years. They are inexpensive, are easy to set up, and are very effective. Plants grow and bud well under them. They are two to three times as efficient as incandescents. Until recently, fluorescents came mostly in straight lengths of 2, 4, 6, or 8 feet, which were placed in standard reflectors. Now there are many more options for the fluorescent user. One of the most convenient fixtures to use is the screw-in converter for use in incandescent sockets, which come with 8 or 12 inch diameter circular fluorescent tubes. A U-shaped 9 inch screw-in fluorescent is also available. Another convenient fixture is the "light wand", which is a 4 foot, very portable tube. It is not saddled with a cumbersome reflector.

Fluorescents come in various spectrums as determined by the type of phosphor with which the surface of the tube is coated. Each phosphor emits a different set of colors. Each tube has a spectrum identification such as "warm white", "cool white", "daylight", or "deluxe cool white" to name a few. This signifies the kind of light the tube produces. For best results, growers use a mixture of tubes which have various shades of white light. One company manufactures a fluorescent tube which is supposed to reproduce the sun's spectrum. It is called Vita-Lite and works well. It comes in a more efficient version, the "Power Twist", which uses the same amount of electricity but emits more light because it has a larger surface area.

"Gro-Tubes" do not work as well as regular fluorescents even though they produce light mainly in the red and blue spectrums. They produce a lot less light than the other tubes.

To maintain a fast growing garden, a minimum of 20 watts of fluorescent light per square foot is required. As long as the plants' other needs are met, the more light that the plants receive, the faster and bushier they will grow. The plants' buds will also be heavier and more developed. Standard straight-tubed fluorescent lamps use 8–10 watts per linear foot. To light a garden, 2 tubes are required for each foot of width. The 8 inch diameter circular tubes use 22 watts, the 12 inch diameter use 32 watts. Using straight tubes, it is possible to fit no more than 4 tubes in each foot of width because of the size of the tubes. A unit using a combination of 8 and 12 inch circular tubes has an input of 54 watts per square foot.

A fluorescent lit garden can produce good buds.

Screw-in fluorescent fixtures are each 8 inches in diameter and use 22 watts. Custom units can be designed to fit odd spaces.

Some companies manufacture energy-saving electronic ballasts designed for use with special fluorescent tubes. These units use 39% less electricity and emit 91% of the light of standard tubes. For instance an Optimizer® warm white 4 foot tube uses 28 watts and emits 2475 lumens.

Both standard and VHO ballasts manufactured before 1980 are not recommended. They were insulated using carcinogenic PCB's and they are a danger to your health should they leak.

The shape of the fluorescent reflector used determines, to a great extent, how much light the plants receive. Fluorescent tubes emit light from their entire surface so that some of the light is directed at the reflector surfaces. Many fixtures place the tubes very close to each other so that only about 40% of the light is actually transmitted out of the unit. The rest of it is trapped between the tubes or between the tubes and the reflector. This light may as well not be emitted since it is doing no good.

A better reflector can be constructed using a wooden frame. Place the tube holders at equal distances from each other at least 4 inches apart. This leaves enough space to construct small mini-reflectors which are angled to reflect the light downward and to separate the light from the different tubes so that it is not lost in crosscurrents. These mini-reflectors can be made from cardboard or plywood and painted white. The units should be no longer than 2½ feet wide so that they can be manipulated easily. Larger units are hard to move up and down and they make access to the garden difficult, especially when the plants are small, and there is not much vertical space. The frame of the reflector should be covered with reflective material such as aluminum foil so that all of the light is directed to the garden. Fluorescent lights should be placed about 2–4 inches from the tops of the plants.

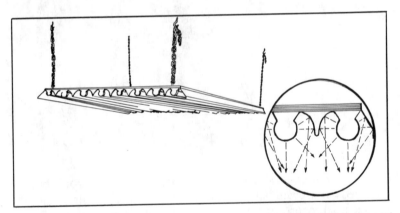

An especially efficient fluorescent reflector unit. Grids between each tube direct the light downward instead of losing it to a horizontal path.

Growers sometimes use fluorescent lights in innovative ways to supplement the main source of light. Lights are sometimes placed along the sides of the garden or in the midst of it. One grower used light wands which he hung vertically in the midst of the garden. This unit provided light to the lower parts of the plants which are often shaded. Another grower hung a tube horizontally at plant level between each row. He used no reflector because the tube shined on the plants from every angle. Lights can be hung at diagonal angles to match the different plants' heights.

VERY HIGH OUTPUT (VHO) FLUORESCENTS

Standard fluorescents use about 10 watts per linear foot—a 4 foot fluorescent uses 40 watts, an 8 footer 72 watts. VHO tubes use about three times the electricity that standard tubes use, or about 215 watts for an 8 foot tube, and they emit about 2½ times the light. While they are not quite as efficient as a standard tube, they are often more convenient to use. Two tubes per foot produce the equivalent electricity of 5 standard tubes. Only one tube per foot is needed and two tubes emit a very bright light. The banks of tubes are eliminated.

VHO tubes come in the same spectrums as standards. They require different ballasts than standards and are available at commercial lighting companies.

When this grower introduced a halide to his garden, he used the spare fluorescents for side-lighting.

For even growth, the plants require equal amounts of light.

This garden in a small room was lit by a single 1000 watt metal halide.

METAL HALIDE LAMPS

Metal halide lamps are probably the most popular lamp used for growing. These are the same type of lamp that are used outdoors as streetlamps or to illuminate sports events. They emit a white light. Metal halide lamps are very convenient to use. They come ready to plug in. The complete unit consists of a lamp (bulb), fixture (reflector) and long cord which plugs into a remote ballast. The fixture and lamp are lightweight and are easy to hang. Only one chain or rope is needed to suspend the fixture, which takes up little space, making it easy to gain access to the garden.

In an unpublished, controlled experiment it was observed that marijuana plants responded better to light if the light came from a single point source such as a metal halide, rather than from emissions from a broad area as with fluorescents. Plants growing under metal halides develop quickly into strong plants. Flowering is profuse, with heavier budding than under fluorescents. Lower leaf development was better too, because the light penetrated the top leaves more.

Metal halide lamps are hung in two configurations: vertical and horizontal. The horizontal lamp easily focuses at a higher percent of light on the garden, but it emits 10% less light. Most manufacturers and distributors sell vertically hanging metal halides. However, it is worth the effort to find a horizontal unit.

A metal halide lamp. Courtesy *Applied Hydroponics,* San Rafael, California.

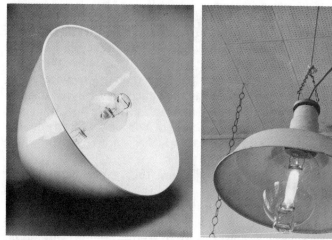

(A)This reflector distributes the light very evenly. Courtesy *Aqua-Culture*, Tempe, Arizona. (B) This reflector loses a lot of light to the side. It is used efficiently only when placed low in a garden of tall plants. Additional reflectors of aluminum foil can modify the unit. Photo by S. Weinstein

Horizontal metal halide lamps emit about 10% less light than vertical lamps, but more of the light emitted by the horizontal lamps is delivered to the garden. According to the manufacturer, this lamp produces 3100 footcandles 1 foot below the reflector vs. 1700 for a vertically mounted lamp. Courtesy *Geotechnology Corp.,* Aromas, California.

In order for a vertical hanging metal halide lamp to deliver light to the garden efficiently, the horizontal light that it is emitting must be directed downward or the halide must be placed in the midst of the garden. It only becomes practical to remove the reflector and let the horizontally directed light radiate when the plants have grown a minimum of six feet tall. Reflectors for vertical lamps should be at least as long as the lamp. If a reflector does not cover the lamp completely, some of the light will be lost horizontally. Many firms sell kits with reflectors which do not cover the whole lamp.

Reflectors can be modified using thin gauge wire such as poultry wire and aluminum foil. A hole is cut out in the middle of the chicken wire frame so that it fits over the wide end of the reflector. Then it is shaped so that it will distribute the light as evenly as possible. Aluminum foil is placed over the poultry wire. (One grower made an outer frame of 1 x 2's which held the poultry wire, metal halide, and foil).

Metal halide lamps come in 400, 1000 and 1500 watt sizes. The 1500 watt lamps are not recommended because they have a much shorter life than the other lamps. The 400 watt lamps can easily illuminate a small garden 5 x 5 feet or smaller. These are ideal lights for a small garden. They are also good to brighten up dark spots in the garden.

In European nurseries, 400 watt horizontal units are standard. They are attached to the ceiling and placed at even 5 foot intervals so that light from several lamps hits each plant. Each lamp beam diffuses as the vertical distance from the plants may be 6–8 feet, but no light is lost. The beams overlap. No shuttle type device is required. The same method can be used with horizontal 1000 watt lamps and 8 foot intervals. Vertical space should be at least 12 feet.

This garden contained 3 lights, 2 metal halide and 1 sodium vapor.

HIGH PRESSURE SODIUM VAPOR LAMPS

Sodium vapor lamps emit an orange or amber-looking light. They are the street lamps that are commonly used these days. These lights look peculiar because they emit a spectrum that is heavily concentrated in the yellow, orange, and red spectrums with only a small amount of blue. They produce about 15% more light than metal halides. They use the same configuration as metal halides: lamp, reflector, and remote ballast.

Growers originally used single sodium vapor lamps primarily for flowering because they thought that if the extra yellow and orange light was closer to the sun's spectrum in the fall, when the amount of blue light reaching Earth was limited, the red light would increase flowering or resin production. In another unpublished controlled experiment, a metal halide lamp and a sodium vapor lamp were used as the only sources of light in 2 different systems. The garden under the metal halide matured about a week faster than the garden under the sodium vapors. Resin content seemed about the same. Other growers have reported different results. They claim that the sodium vapor lamp does increase THC and resin production. Plants can be grown under sodium vapor lights as the sole source of illumination.

Many growers use sodium vapor lamps in conjunction with metal halides; a typical ratio is 2 halides to 1 sodium. Some growers use metal halides during the growth stages but change to sodium vapor lamps during the harvest cycle. This is not hard to do since both lamps fit in the same reflector. The lamps use different ballasts.

High pressure sodium vapor lamps come in 400 and 1000 watt configurations with remote ballasts designed specifically for cultivation. Smaller wattages designed for outdoor illumination are available from hardware stores. The small wattage lamps can be used for brightening dark areas of the garden or for hanging between the rows of plants in order to provide bright light below the tops.

The wide lamp reflector helps to distribute the light evenly throughout the growing space. Courtesy *Hydro-Tech*, Seattle, Washington.

Sun Circle™ moves lamps 'round and round' at one revolution every 40 minutes. When HPS and MH lamps are rotated together, the entire growing area receives equal illumination from both lamps. A slip clutch permits manual movement of lamps to facilitate garden maintenance. Courtesy *Sun Circle*, Ferndale, California.

ACCESSORIES

One of the most innovative accessories for lighting is the "Solar Shuttle"® and its copies. This device moves a metal halide or sodium vapor lamp across a track 6 feet or longer. Because the lamp is moving, each plant comes directly under its field several times during the growing period. Instead of plants in the center receiving more light than those on the edge, the light is more equally distributed. This type of unit increases the total efficiency of the light. Garden space can be increased by 15-20% or the lamp can be used to give the existing garden more light.

Other units move the lamps over an arc path. The units take various amounts of time to complete a journey — from 40 seconds upward.

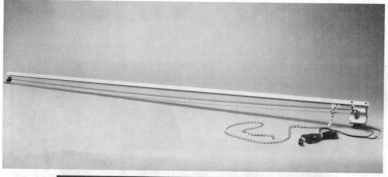

The Solar Shuttle® moves a single light back and forth over a 6 foot track. A round trip takes about 40 minutes. Inset is closeup of unit. Courtesy *Aqua Culture*, Tempe, Arizona.

ELECTRICITY AND LIGHTING

At 110–120 volts, a 1000 watt lamp uses about 8.7 amps (watts divided by volts equals amps). Including a 15% margin for safety it can be figured as 10 amps. Many household circuits are rated for 20 or 30 amps. Running 2 lights on a twenty amp circuit taxes it to capacity and is dangerous. If more electricity is required than can be safely supplied on a circuit, new wiring can be installed from the fusebox.

All electrical equipment should be grounded.

Some growers report that the electrical company's interest was aroused, sometimes innocently, when their electric bill began to spurt. After all, each hour a lamp is on it uses about 1 kilowatt hour.

Chapter Twelve
Carbon Dioxide

Carbon dioxide (CO_2) is a gas which comprises about .03% or (300 parts per million, "PPM") of the atmosphere. It is not dangerous. It is one of the basic raw materials (water is the other) required for photosynthesis. The plant makes a sugar molecule using light for energy, CO_2 which is pulled out of the air, and water, which is pulled up from its roots.

Scientists believe that early in the Earth's history the atmosphere contained many times the amount of CO_2 it does today. Plants have never lost their ability to process gas at these high rates. In fact, with the Earth's present atmosphere, plant growth is limited.

When plants are growing in an enclosed area, there is a limited amount of CO_2 for them to use. When the CO_2 is used up, the plant's photosynthesis stops. Only as more CO_2 is provided can the plant use light to continue the process. Adequate amounts of CO_2 may be easily replaced in well-ventilated areas, but increasing the amount of CO_2 to .2% (2000 PPM) or 6 times the amount usually found in the atmosphere, can increase the growth rate by up to 5 times. For this reason, many commercial nurseries provide a CO_2-enriched area for their plants.

Luckily, CO_2 can be supplied cheaply. At the most organic level, there are many metabolic processes that create CO_2. For example, organic gardeners sometimes make compost in the greenhouse. About ⅙ to ¼ of the pile's starting wet weight is converted to CO_2 so that a 200 pound pile contributes 33–50 pounds of carbon to the gas. Carbon makes up about 27% of the weight and volume of the gas and oxygen makes up 73%, so that the total amount of CO_2 created is 122 to 185 pounds produced over a 30 day period.

Brewers and vintners would do well to ferment their beverages in the greenhouse. Yeast eat the sugars contained in the fermentation mix, releasing CO_2 and alcohol. The yeast produce quite a bit of CO_2 when they are active.

One grower living in a rural area has some rabbit hutches in his greenhouse. The rabbits use the oxygen produced by the plants, and in return, release CO_2 by breathing. Another grower told me that he is supplying his plants with CO_2 by spraying them periodically with seltzer (salt-free soda water), which is water with CO_2 dissolved. He claims to double the plants' growth rate. This method is a bit expensive when the plants are large, but economical when they are small.

A correspondent used the exhausts from his gas-fired water heater and clothes dryer. To make the area safe of toxic fumes that might be in the exhaust, he built a manually operated shut-off valve so that the spent air could be directed into the growing chamber or up a flue. Before he entered the room he sent any exhausts up the flue and turned on a ventilating fan which drew air out of the room.

Growers do not have to become brewers, rabbit farmers, or spray their plants with Canada Dry®. There are several economical and convenient ways to give the plants adequate amounts of CO_2: using a CO_2 generator, which burns natural gas or kerosene, using a CO_2 tank with regulator, or by evaporating dry ice.

To find out how much CO_2 is needed to bring the growing area to the ideal 2000 PPM, multiply the cubic area of the growing room (length x width x height) by .002. The total represents the number of square feet of gas required to reach optimum CO_2 range. For instance, a room 13' x 18' x 12' contains 2808 cubic feet: 2808 x .002 equals 5.6 cubic feet of CO_2 required. The easiest way to supply the gas is to use a CO_2 tank. All the equipment can be built from parts available at a welding supply store or purchased totally assembled from many growing supply companies. Usually tanks come in 20 and 50 pound sizes, and can be bought or rented. A tank which holds 50 pounds has a gross weight of 170 pounds when filled.

A grow room of 500 cubic feet requires 1 cubic foot of CO_2
A grow room of 1000 cubic feet requires 2 cubic feet of CO_2
A grow room of 5000 cubic feet requires 10 cubic feet of CO_2
A grow room of 10,000 cubic feet requires 20 cubic feet of CO_2

To regulate dispersal of the gas, a combination flow meter/regulator is required. Together they regulate the flow between 10 and 50 cubic feet per hour. The regulator standardizes the pressure and regulates the number of cubic feet released per hour. A solenoid valve shuts the flow meter on and off as regulated by a multicycle timer, so the valve can be turned on and off several times

A CO₂ commercial regulator. This unit controls intake and exhaust blowers too. Courtesy *Emerald City Halide,* Seattle, Washington.

Units similar to this can be constructed by the home hobbyist using a meter, regulator and solenoid valve on a timer. This early commercial unit is no longer available. Courtesy *Applied Hydroponics,* San Rafael, California.

each day. If the growing room is small, a short-range timer is needed. Most timers are calibrated in ½ hour increments, but a short-range timer keeps the valve open only a few minutes.

To find out how long the valve should remain open, the number of cubic feet of gas required (in our example 5.6 cubic feet) is divided by the flow rate. For instance, if the flow rate is 10 cubic feet per hour, 5.6 divided by 10 = .56 hours or 33 minutes (.56 × 60 minutes = 33 minutes). At 30 cubic feet per hour, the number of minutes would be .56 divided by 30 × 60 minutes = 11.2 minutes.

The gas should be replenished every two hours in a warm, well-lit room when the plants are over 3 feet high if there is no outside ventilation. When the plants are smaller or in a moderately lit room, they do not use the CO_2 as fast. With ventilation the gas should be replenished once an hour or more frequently. Some growers have a ventilation fan on a timer in conjunction with the gas. The fan goes off when the gas is injected into the room. A few minutes before the gas is injected in the room, the fan starts and removes the old air. The gas should be released above the plants since the gas is heavier than air and sinks. A good way to disperse the gas is by using inexpensive "soaker hoses", sold in plant nurseries. These soaker hoses have tiny holes in them to let out the CO_2.

The CO_2 tank is placed where it can be removed easily. A hose is run from the regulator unit (where the gas comes out) to the top of the garden. CO_2 is cooler and heavier than air and will flow downward, reaching the top of the plants first.

This CO_2 enrichment system is very effective and is simple to operate. It adjusts the flow rate and timing very easily. Courtesy *Applied Hydroponics*, San Rafael, California.

Dry ice is CO_2 which has been cooled to -109 degrees, at which temperature it becomes a solid. It costs about the same as the gas in tanks. It usually comes in 30 pound blocks which evaporate at the rate of about 7% a day when kept in a freezer. At room temperatures, the gas evaporates considerably faster, probably supplying much more CO_2 than is needed by the plants. One grower worked at a packing plant where dry ice was used. Each day he took home a couple of pounds, which fit into his lunch pail. When he came home he put the dry ice in the grow room, where it evaporated over the course of the day.

Gas and kerosene generators work by burning hydrocarbons which release heat and create CO_2 and water. Each pound of fuel burned produces about 3 pounds of CO_2, 1½ pounds of water and about 21,800 BTU's (British Thermal Units) of heat. Some gases and other fuels may have less energy (BTU's) per pound. The fuel's BTU rating is checked before making calculations.

Nursery supply houses sell CO_2 generators especially designed for greenhouses, but household style kerosene or gas heaters are also suitable. They need no vent. The CO_2 goes directly into the room's atmosphere. Good heaters burn cleanly and completely, leaving no residues, creating no carbon monoxide (a colorless, odorless, poisonous gas). Even so, it is a good idea to shut the heater off and vent the room before entering the space.

If a heater is not working correctly, most likely it burns the fuel incompletely, creating an odor. More expensive units have pilots and timers; less expensive models must be adjusted manually. Heaters with pilots can be modified to use a solenoid valve and timer.

At room temperature, one pound of CO_2 equals 8.7 cubic feet. It takes only ⅓ of a pound of kerosene (5.3 ounces) to make a pound of CO_2. To calculate the amount of fuel required, the number of cubic feet of gas desired is divided by 8.7 and multiplied by .33. In our case, 5.6 cubic feet divided by 8.7 times .33 equals .21 pounds of fuel. To find out how many ounces this is, multiply .21 times 16 (number of ounces in a pound) to arrive at a total of 3.3 ounces, a little less than half a cup (4 ounces).

$\frac{6}{10}$ths ounce produces 1 cubic foot of CO_2
1.2 ounces produce 2 cubic feet of CO_2
3 ounces produce 5 cubic feet of CO_2
6 ounces produce 10 cubic feet of CO_2

A simple gas heater and propane tank can be used to heat the garden as it provides CO_2.
Photo by S. Weinstein

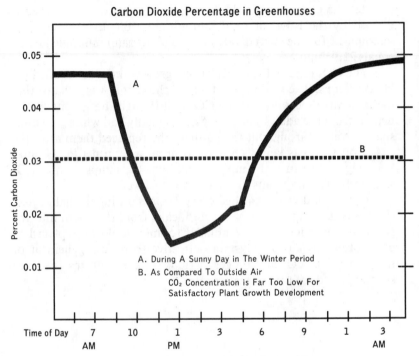

Carbon Dioxide Percentage in Greenhouses

A. During A Sunny Day in The Winter Period
B. As Compared To Outside Air
   CO₂ Concentration is Far Too Low For
   Satisfactory Plant Growth Development

Courtesy, Sylvania Lighting Products, Danvers, Mass.
Bulletin #0-352, p. 4.

To find out fuel usage, divide the number of BTU's produced by 21,800. If a generator produces 12,000 BTU's an hour, it is using 12,000 divided by 21,800 or about .55 pounds of fuel per hour. However only .21 pounds are needed. To calculate the number of minutes the generator should be on, the amount of fuel needed is divided by the flow rate and multiplied by 60. In our case, .21 (amount of fuel needed) divided by .55 (flow rate) multiplied by 60 equals 22.9 minutes.

The CO_2 required for at least one grow room was supplied using gas lamps. The grower said that she thought it was a shame that the fuel was used only for the CO_2 and thought her plants would benefit from the additional light. She originally had white gas lamps spaced evenly throughout the garden. She replaced them after the first crop with gas lamps all hooked up to a central LP gas tank. She only had to turn the unit on and light the lamps each day. It shut itself off. She claims the system worked well.

CO_2 should be replenished every 3 hours during the light cycle, since it is used up by the plants and leaks from the room into the general atmosphere. Well-ventilated rooms should be replenished more often. It is probably more effective to have a generator or tank releasing CO_2 for longer periods at slower rates than for shorter periods of time at higher rates.

Chapter Thirteen
Temperature

Marijuana plants are very hardy and survive over a wide range of temperatures. They can withstand extremely hot weather, up to 120 degrees, as long as they have adequate supplies of water. Cannabis seedlings regularly survive light frost at the beginning of the season.

Both high and low temperatures slow marijuana's rate of metabolism and growth. The plants function best in moderate temperatures — between 60 and 85 degrees. As more light is available, the ideal temperature for normal plant growth increases. If plants are given high temperatures and only moderate light, the stems elongate. Conversely, strong light and low temperatures decrease stem elongation. During periods of low light, strong elongation is decreased by lowering the temperature. Night temperatures should be 10–15 degrees lower than daytime temperatures.

Temperatures below 50 degrees slow growth of most varieties. When the temperature goes below 40 degrees, the plants may experience some damage and require about 24 hours to resume growth. Low nighttime temperatures may delay or prevent bud maturation. Some equatorial varieties stop growth after a few 40 degree nights.

A sunny room or one illuminated by high wattage lamps heats up rapidly. During the winter the heat produced may keep the room comfortable. However the room may get too warm during the summer. Heat rises, so that the temperature is best measured at the plants' height. A room with a 10 foot ceiling may feel uncomfortably warm at head level but be fine for plants 2 feet tall.

If the room has a vent or window, an exhaust fan can be used to cool it. Totally enclosed spaces can be cooled using a water conditioner which cools the air by evaporating water. If the room is lit entirely by lamps, the day/night cycle can be reversed so that the heat is generated at night, when it is cooler out.

Marijuana is low-temperature tolerant. Outdoors, seedlings sometimes pierce snow cover, and older plants can withstand short, light frosts. Statistically, more males develop in cold temperatures. However, low temperatures slow down the rate of plant metabolism. Cold floors lower the temperature in containers and medium, slowing germination and growth. Ideally, the medium temperature should be 70 degrees. There are several ways to warm the medium. The floor can be insulated using a thin sheet of styrofoam, foam rubber, wood or newspaper. The best way to in- sulate a container from a cold floor is to raise the container so that there is an air space between it and the floor.

Overhead fans, which circulate the warm air downward from the top of the room also warm the medium.

When the plants' roots are kept warm, the rest of the plant can be kept cooler with no damage. Heat cables or heat mats, which use small amounts of electricity, can be used to heat the root area. These are available at nursery supply houses.

When watering, tepid water should be used. Cultivators using systems that recirculate water can heat the water with a fish tank heater and thermostat. If the air is cool, 45–60 degrees, the water can be heated to 90 degrees. If the air is warm, over 60 degrees, 70 degrees for the water is sufficient. The pipes and medium absorb the water down a bit before it reaches the roots.

Gardens using artificial lighting can generate high air temperatures. Each 1000 watt metal halide and ballast emits just a little less energy than a 10 amp heater. Several lights can raise the temperature to an intolerable level. In this case a heat exchanger is required. A venting fan or misters can be used to lower temperatures. Misters are not recommended for use around lights.

Greenhouses can also get very hot during the summer. If the sun is very bright, opaquing paint may lower the amount of light and heat entering the greenhouse. Fans and cooling mats also help. Cooling mats are fibrous plastic mats which hold moisture. Fans blow air through the mats which lowers the greenhouse temperature. They are most effective in hot dry areas. They are available through nursery supply houses.

Chapter Fourteen
Air and Humidity

Besides temperature and CO_2 content, air has other qualities including dust content, electrical charge and humidity.

Dust

"Dust" is actually composed of many different-sized solid and liquid particles which float in the gaseous soup. The particles include organic fibers, hair, other animal and vegetable particles, bacteria, viruses, smoke and odoriferous liquid particles such as essential oils, and water-soluble condensates. Virtually all of the particles have a positive electrical charge, which means that they are missing an electron, and they float (due to electrical charge) through various passing gasses.

The dust content of the air affects the efficiency of the plant's ability to photosynthesize. Although floating dust may block a small amount of light, dust which has precipitated on leaves may block large amounts. Furthermore, the dust clogs the pores through which plants transpire. Dust can easily be washed off leaves using a fine mist spray. Water must be prevented from touching and shattering the hot glass of the lights.

Negative Ions

In unindustrialized verdant areas and near large bodies of water, the air is negatively charged, that is, there are electrons floating in the air unattached to atoms or molecules. In industrialized areas or very dry regions, the air is positively charged; there are atoms and molecules missing electrons.

Some researchers claim that the air's electrical charge affects plant growth (and also animal behavior). They claim that plants in a positively charged environment grow slower than those in a negatively charged area.

Regardless of the controversy regarding growth and the air's electrical charge, the presence of negative ions creates some readily observable effects. Odors are characteristic of positively charged particles floating in the air. A surplus of negative ions causes the particles to precipitate so that there are no odors. With enough negative ions, a room filled with pungent, flowering sinsemilla is odorless.

Spaces with a "surplus" negative ion charge have clean, fresh-smelling air. Falling water, which generates negative ions, characteristically creates refreshing air. Dust particles are precipitated so that there are fewer bacteria and fungus spores floating in the air, as well as much less dust in general. This lowers chance of infection.

Many firms manufacture "Negative Ion Generators", "Ionizers", and "Ion Fountains", which disperse large quantities of negative ions into the atmosphere. These units are inexpensive, safe and recommended for all growing areas. Ion generators precipitate particles floating in the air. With most generators, the precipitating particles land within a radius of two feet of the point of dispersal, collecting quickly and developing into a thick film of grime. Newspaper is placed around the unit so that the space does not get soiled. Some newer units have a precipitator which collects dust on a charged plate instead of the other surrounding surfaces. This plate can be roughly simulated by grounding a sheet of aluminum foil. To ground foil, either attach it directly to a metal plumbing line or grounding box; for convenience, the foil can be held with an alligator clip attached to the electrical wire, which is attached to the grounding source. As the foil gets soiled, it is replaced.

Humidity

Cannabis grows best in a mildly humid environment: a relative humidity of 40–60 percent. Plants growing in drier areas may experience chronic wilt and necrosis of the leaf tips. Plants growing in a wetter environment usually experience few problems; however, the buds are more susceptible to molds which can attack a garden overnight and ruin a crop.

Growers are rarely faced with too dry a growing area. Since the space is enclosed, water which is evaporated or transpired by the plants increases the humidity considerably. If there is no ventilation, a large space may reach saturation level within a few days. Smaller spaces usually do not have this buildup because there is usually enough air movement to dissipate the humidity. The solution may be as easy as opening a window. A small ventilation fan can move quite a bit of air out of a space and may be a convenient way of solving the problem. Humidity may be removed using a dehumidifier in gardens without access to convenient ventilation.

Dehumidifiers work the same way a refrigerator does except that instead of cooling a space, a series of tubes is cooled causing atmospheric water to condense. The smallest dehumidifiers (which can dry out a large space) use about 15 amps. Usually the dehumidifier needs to run only a few hours a day. If the plant regimen includes a dark cycle, then the dehumidifier can be run when the lights are off, to ease the electrical load.

Air Circulation

A close inspection of a marijuana leaf reveals many tiny hairs and a rough surface. Combined, these trap air and create a micro-environment around the plant. The trapped air contains more humidity and oxygen and is warmer, which differs significantly in composition and temperature from the surrounding atmosphere. The plant uses CO_2 so there is less left in the air surrounding the leaf. Marijuana depends on air currents to move this air and renew the micro-environment. If the air is not moved vigorously, the growth rate slows, since the micro-environment becomes CO_2 depleted.

Plants develop firm, sturdy stems as the result of environmental stresses. Outdoors, the plants sway with the wind, causing tiny breaks in the stem. These are quickly repaired by the plant's reinforcing the original area and leaving it stronger than it was originally. Indoors, plants don't usually need to cope with these stresses so their stems grow weak unless the plants receive a breeze or are shaken by the stems daily.

A steady air flow from outdoor ventilation may be enough to keep the air moving. If this is not available, a revolving fan placed several feet from the nearest plant or a slow-moving overhead fan can solve the problem. Screen all air intake fans to prevent pests.

Chapter Fifteen
pH and Water

The pH is the measure of acid-alkalinity balance of a solution. It is measured on a scale of 0–14, with 0 being the most acid, 7 being neutral, and 14 being most alkaline. Most nutrients the plants use are soluble only in a limited range of acidity, between about 6 to about 7½, neutral. Should the water become too acid or alkaline, the nutrients dissolved in the water precipitate and become unavailable to the plants. When the nutrients are locked up, plant growth is slowed. Typically, a plant growing in an environment with a low pH will be very small, often growing only a few inches in several months. Plants growing in a high pH environment will look pale and sickly and also have stunted growth.

All water has a pH which can be measured using aquarium or garden pH chemical reagent test kits or a pH meter. All of these items are available at local stores and are easy to use. Water is pH-adjusted after nutrients are added, since nutrients affect the pH.

Once the water is tested it should be adjusted if it does not fall within the pH range of 6 to 7. Ideally the range should be about 6.2–6.8. Hydroponic supply companies sell measured adjusters which are very convenient and highly recommended. The water-nutrient solution can be adjusted using common household chemicals. Water which is too acid can be neutralized using bicarbonate of soda, wood ash, or by using a solution of lime in the medium.

Water which is too alkaline can be adjusted using nitric acid, sulfuric acid, citric acid (Vitamin C) or vinegar. The water is adjusted using small increments of chemicals. Once a standard measure of how much chemical is needed to adjust the water, the process becomes fast and easy to do.

Plants affect the pH of the water solution as they remove various nutrients which they use. Microbes growing in the medium also change the pH. For this reason growers check and adjust the pH periodically, about once every two weeks.

The pH of water out of the tap may change with the season so it is a good idea to test it periodically.

Some gardeners let tap water sit for a day so that the chlorine evaporates. They believe that chlorine is harmful to plants.

The pH of the planting medium affects the pH of the liquid in solution. Medium should be adjusted so that it tests between 6.2-6.8. This is done before the containers are filled so that the medium could be adjusted in bulk. Approximately 1-2 lbs. of dolomitic limestone raises the pH of 100 gallons (4.5-9 grams per gallon) of soil 1 point. Gypsum can be used to lower the pH of soil or medium. Both limestone and gypsum have limited solubility.

There are many forms of limestone which have various effectiveness depending on their chemistry. Each has a rating on the package.

Chapter Sixteen

Nutrients

Marijuana requires a total of 14 nutrients which it obtains through its roots. Nitrogen (N), Phosphorous (P), and Potassium (K) are called the macro-nutrients because they are used in large quantities by the plant. The percentages of N, P, and K are always listed in the same order on fertilizer packages.

Calcium (Ca), sulfur (S), and magnesium (Mg) are also required by the plants in fairly large quantities. These are often called the secondary nutrients.

Smaller amounts of iron (Fe), zinc (Zn), manganese (Mn), boron (B), cobalt (Co), copper (Cu), molybdenum (Mo) and chlorine (Cl) are also needed. These are called micro-nutrients.

Marijuana requires more N before flowering than later in its cycle. When it begins to flower, marijuana's use of P increases. Potassium requirements increase after plants are fertilized as a result of seed production.

Plants which are being grown in soil mixes or mixes with nutrients added such as compost, manure or time-release fertilizers may need no additional fertilizing or only supplemental amounts if the plants begin to show deficiencies.

The two easiest and most reliable ways to meet the plant's needs are to use a prepared hydroponic fertilizer or an organic water-soluble fertilizer. Hydroponic fertilizers are blended as complete balanced formulas. Most non-hydroponic fertilizers usually contain only the macronutrients, N, P and K. Organic fertilizers such as fish emulsion and other blends contain trace elements which are found in the organic matter from which they are derived.

Most indoor plant fertilizers are water-soluble. A few of them are time-release formulas which are mixed into the medium as it is being prepared. Plants grown in soil mixes can usually get along using regular fertilizers but plants grown in prepared soilless mixes definitely require micronutrients.

As the seeds germinate they are given a nutrient solution high in N such as a 20–10–10 or 17–10–12. These are just two possible formulas; any with a high proportion of N will do.

Formulas which are not especially high in N can be used and supplemented with a high N fertilizer such as fish emulsion (which may create an odor) or the Sudbury X® component fertilizer which is listed as 44-0-0. Urine is also very high in N and is easily absorbed by the plants. It should be diluted to one cup urine per gallon of water.

The plants should be kept on a high N fertilizer regimen until they are put into the flowering regimen.

During the flowering cycle, the plants do best with a formula lower in N and higher in P, which promotes bloom. A fertilizer such as 5-20-10 or 10-19-12 will do. (Once again, these are typical formulas, similar ones will do).

Growers who make their own nutrient mixes based on parts per million of nutrient generally use the following formulas.

CHART 15-1: NUTRIENT/WATER SOLUTION IN PARTS PER MILLION (PPM)

	N	P	K
Germination - 15 to 20 days	110-150	70-100	50-75
Fast Growth	200-250	60-80	150-200
Pre-Flowering 2 weeks before turning light down	70-100	100-150	75-100
Flowering	0-50	100-150	50-75
Seeding - fertilized flowers	100-200	70-100	100-150

Plants can be grown using a nutrient solution containing no N for the last 10 days. Many of the larger leaves yellow and wither as the N migrates from old to the new growth. The buds are less green and have less of a minty (chlorophyll) taste.

Many cultivators use several brands and formulas of fertilizer. They either mix them together in solution or switch brands each feeding.

Plant N requirements vary by weather as well as growth cycle. Plants growing under hot conditions are given 10-20% less N or else they tend to elongate and to grow thinner, weaker stalks. Plants in a cool or cold regimen may be given 10-20% more N. More N is given under high light conditions, less is used under low light conditions.

Organic growers can make "teas" from organic nutrients by soaking them in water. Organic nutrients usually contain micronutrients as well as the primary ones. Manures and blood meal are among the most popular organic teas, but other organic sources of nutrients include urine, which may be the best source for N, as well as blood meal and tankage. Organic fertilizers vary in their formulas. The exact formula is usually listed on the label.

Here is a list of common organic fertilizers which can be used to make teas:

CHART 15-2: ORGANIC FERTILIZERS

Fertilizer	N	P	K	Remarks
Bloodmeal	15	1.3	.7	Releases nutrients easily
Cow manure (dried)	1.5	.85	1.75	The classic tea. Well-balanced formula. Medium availability.
Dried blood	13	3	0	Nutrients dissolve easier than bloodmeal.
Chicken manure	3.5	1.5	.85	Excellent nutrients.
Wood ashes	0	1.5	7	Water-soluble. Very alkaline except with acid wood such as walnut.
Granite dust	0	0	5	Dissolves slowly
Rock phospate (phosphorous)	0	33	0	Dissolves gradually.
Urine (human, fresh)	.5	.003	.003	N immediately available.

Commercial water-soluble fertilizers are available. Fish emulsion fertilizer comes in 5-1-1 and 5-2-2 formulas and has been used by satisfied growers for years.

A grower cannot go wrong changing hydroponic water/nutrient solutions at least once a month. Once every two weeks is even better. The old solution could be measured, reformulated, supplemented and re-used; unless large amounts of fertilizer are used, such as in a large commercial greenhouse, it is not worth the effort. The old solution may have many nutrients left, but it may be unbalanced since the plants have drawn specific chemicals. The water can be used to water houseplants or an outdoor garden, or to enrich a compost pile.

Experienced growers fertilize by eyeing the plants and trying to determine their needs when minor symptoms of deficiencies become apparent. If the nutrient added cures the deficiency, the plant usually responds in apparent ways within one or two days. First the spread of the symptom stops. With some minerals, plant parts that were not too badly damaged begin to repair themselves. Plant parts which were slightly discolored may return to normal. Plant parts which were severely damaged or suffered from necrosis do not recover. The most dramatic changes usually appear in new growth. These parts grow normally. A grower can tell just by plant parts which part grew before deficiencies were corrected.

Fertilizers should be applied on the low side of recommended rates. Overdoses quickly (within hours) result in wilting and then death. The symptoms are a sudden wilt with leaves curled under. To save plants suffering from toxic overdoses of nutrients, plain water is run through systems to wash out the medium.

Gardens with drainage can be cared for using a method commercial nurseries employ. The plants are watered each time with a dilute nutrient/water solution, usually 20-25% of full strength. Excess water runs off. While this method uses more water and nutrients than other techniqes, it is easy to set up and maintain.

When nutrient deficiencies occur, especially multiple or micronutrient deficiencies, there is a good chance that the minerals are locked up (precipitated) because of pH. Rather than just adding more nutrients, the pH must be checked first. If needed, the pH must be changed by adjusting the water.

If the pH is too high, the water is made a lower pH than it would ordinarily be; if too low the water is made a higher pH. To get nutrients to the plant parts immediately, a dilute foliar spray is used. If the plant does not respond to the foliar spray, it is being treated with the wrong nutrient.

NUTRIENTS

Nitrogen (N)

Marijuana uses more N than any other nutrient. It is used in the manufacture of chlorophyll. N migrates from old growth to new, so that a shortage is likely to cause first pale green leaves and then the yellowing and withering of the lowest leaves as the nitrogen travels to new buds. Other deficiency symptoms include smaller leaves, slow growth and a sparse rather than bushy profile.

N-deficient plants respond quickly to fertilization. Within a day or two, pale leaves become greener and the rate and size of new growth increases. Good water-soluble sources of nitrogen include most indoor and hydroponic fertilizers, fish emulsion, and urine, along with teas made from manures, dried blood or bloodmeal. There are many organic additives which release N over a period of time that can be added to the medium at the time of planting. These include manures, blood, cottonseed meal, hair, fur, or tankage.

Phosphorous (P)

P is used by plants in the transfer of light energy to chemical compounds. It is also used in large quantities for root growth and flowering. Marijuana uses P mostly during early growth and flowering.

Fertilizers and nutrient mixes usually supply adequate amounts of P during growth stages so plants usually do not experience a deficiency. Rock phosphate and bone meal are the organic fertilizers usually recommended for P deficiency. However they release the mineral slowly, and are more suited to outdoor gardening than indoors. They can be added to mediums to supplement soluble fertilizers.

P-deficient plants have small dark green leaves, with red stems and red veins. The tips of lower leaves sometimes die. Eventually the entire lower leaves yellow and die. Fertilization affects only new growth.

Marijuana uses large quantities of P during flowering. Many fertilizer manufacturers sell mixes high in P specifically for blooming plants.

Potassium (K)

K is used by plants to regulate carbohydrate metabolism, chlorophyll synthesis, and protein synthesis as well as to provide resistance to disease. Adequate amounts of K result in strong, sturdy stems while slightly deficient plants often grow taller, thinner stems. Plants producing seed use large amounts of K. Breeding plants can be given K supplements to assure well-developed seed.

Symptoms of greater deficiencies are more apparent on the sun leaves (the large lower leaves). Necrotic patches are found on the leaf tips and then in patches throughout the leaf. The leaves also look pale green.

Stems and flowers on some plants turn deep red or purple as a result of K deficiencies. However, red stems are a genetic characteristic of some plants so this symptom is not foolproof. Outdoors, a cold spell can precipitate K and make it unavailable to the plants, so that almost overnight the flowers and stems turn purple.

K deficiency can be treated with any high-K fertilizer. Old growth does not absorb the nutrient and will not be affected. However, new growth will show no signs of deficiency within 2 weeks. For faster results the fertilizer can be used as a foliar spray. K deficiency does not seem to be a crucial problem. Except for the few symptoms, plants do not seem to be affected by it.

Calcium (Ca)

Ca is used during cell splitting, and to build the cell membranes. Marijuana also stores "excess" Ca for reasons unknown. I have never seen a case of Ca deficiency in cannabis. Soils and fertilizers usually contain adequate amounts. It should be added to planting mixes when they are being formulated at the rate of 1 tablespoon per gallon or ½ cup per cubic foot of medium.

Sulfur (S)

S is used by the plant to help regulate metabolism, and as a constituent of some vitamins, amino acids and proteins. It is plentiful in soil and hydroponic mixes.

S deficiencies are rare. First, new growth yellows and the entire plant pales.

S deficiencies are easily solved using Epsom salts at the rate of 1 tablespoon per gallon of water.

Magnesium (Mg)

Mg is the central atom in chlorophyll and is also used in production of carbohydrates. (Chlorophyll looks just like hemoglobin in blood, but has a Mg atom. Hemoglobin has an Fe atom). In potted plants, Mg deficiency is fairly common, since many otherwise well-balanced fertilizers do not contain it.

Deficiency symptoms start on the lower leaves which turn yellow, leaving only the veins green. The leaves curl up and die along the tips and edges. Growing shoots are pale green and, as the condition continues, turn almost white.

Mg deficiency is easily treated using Epsom salts ($MgSO_4$) at the rate of 1 tablespoon per gallon of water. For faster results, a foliar spray is used. Once Mg deficiency occurs, Epsom salts should be added to the solution each time it is changed. Dolomitic limestone contains large amounts of Mg.

Iron (Fe)

Fe deficiency is not uncommon. The growing shoots are pale or white, leaving only dark green veins. The symptoms appear similar to Mg deficiencies but Fe deficiencies do not affect the lower leaves. Fe deficiencies are often the result of acid-alkalinity imbalances.

Fe deficiencies sometimes occur together with zinc (Zn) and manganese (Mn) deficiencies so that several symptoms appear simultaneously.

Deficiencies can be corrected by adjusting the pH, adding rusty water to the medium, or using a commercial supplement. Fe supplements are sold alone or in a mix combined with Zn and Mn. To prevent deficiencies, some growers add a few rusting nails to each container. One grower using a reservoir system added a pound of nails to the holding tank. The nails added Fe to the nutrient solution as they rusted. Dilute foliar sprays can be used to treat deficiencies.

Manganese (Mn)

Symptoms of Mn deficiency include yellowing and dying of tissue between veins, first appearing on new growth and then throughout the plant.

Deficiencies are solved using an Fe-Zn-Mn supplement.

Zinc (Zn)

Zn deficiency is noted first as yellowing and necrosis of older leaf margins and tips and then as twisted, curled new growth. Treatment with a Fe-Zn-Mn supplement quickly relieves symptoms. A foliar spray speeds the nutrients to the leaf tissue.

Boron (B)

B deficiency is uncommon and does not usually occur indoors.

Symptoms of B deficiency start at the growing tips, which turn grey or brown and then die. This spreads to the lateral shoots.

A B deficiency is treated by using ½ teaspoon boric acid, available in pharmacies, added to a gallon of water. One treatment is usually sufficient.

Molybdenum (Mo)

Mo is used by plants in the conversion of N to forms that the plant can use. It is also a constituent of some enzymes. Deficiency is unusual indoors.

Symptoms start with paleness, then yellowing of middle leaves which progress to the new shoots and growing tips, which grow twisted. The early symptoms almost mimic N deficiency. Treatment with N may temporarily relieve the symptoms but they return within a few weeks.

Mo is included in hydroponic fertilizers and in some trace element mixes. It can be used as a foliar spray.

Copper (Cu)

Cu is used by plants in the transfer of electrical charges which are manipulated by the plant to absorb nutrients and water. It is also used in the regulation of water content and is a constituent of some enzymes.

Cu deficiencies are rare and mimic symptoms of overfertilization. The leaves are limp and turn under at the edges. Tips and edges of the leaves may die and whole plant looks wilted.

A fungicide, copper sulfate, ($CuSO_4$) can be used as a foliar spray to relieve the deficiency.

98

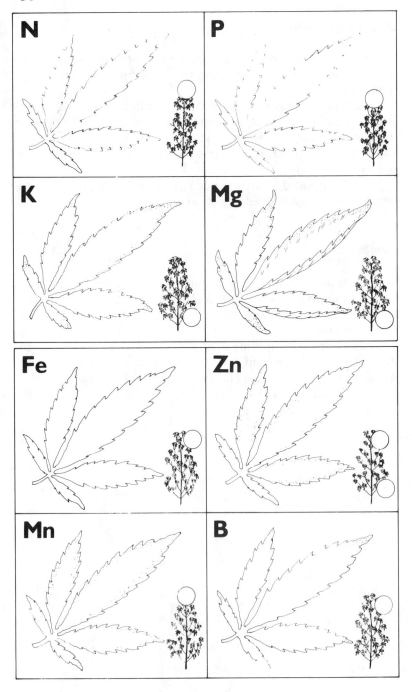

DEFICIENCIES OF NUTRIENT ELEMENTS IN MARIJUANA

Symptoms	N	P	K	Mg	Fe	Cu	Zn	B	Mo	Mn	Over Fertilization
Yellowing of:											
Younger leaves					X					X	
Middle leaves								X			
Older leaves	X		X	X			X				
Between veins				X						X	
Old leaves drop	X										
Leaf Curl Over				X							
Leaf Curl Under			X			X					X
Leaf tips burn											
Younger leaves								X			
Older leaves	X						X				
Young leaves wrinkle & curl			X				X	X	X		
Necrosis			X	X	X		X			X	
Leaf growth stunted	X	X									
Dark green/purplish leaves and stems		X									
Pale green leaf color	X								X		
Mottling							X				
Spindly	X										
Soft stems	X		X								
Hard/brittle stems		X	X								
Growing tips die			X					X			
Stunted root growth		X									
Wilting						X					

KEY TO NUTRIENT DEFICIENCY ILLUSTRATION

Yellow	Pale Green	Dark Green	Purple	Dead

NUTRIENT ADDITIVES

Various additives are often suggested to boost the nutrient value of the water/nutrient solution. Here are some of them:

WETTING AGENTS. Water holds together through surface tension, preventing it from dispersing easily over dry surfaces. Wetting agents decrease the surface tension and allow the water to easily penetrate evenly throughout the medium, preventing dry spots. Wetting agents are helpful when they are used with fresh medium and as an occasional additive. Wetting agents should not be used on a regular basis. They may interfere with plants' ability to grow root hairs, which are ordinarily found on the roots. They are available at most plant nurseries.

SEAWEED. Washed, ground seaweed contains many trace elements and minerals used by plants. It may also contain some hormones or organic nutrients not yet identified.

KELP. Kelp seems to be similar to seaweed in nutrient value. Proponents claim that it has other, as yet undefined organic chemicals that boost plant growth.

SEA WATER. Salt water contains many trace elements and organic compounds. Some hydroponists claim that adding 5-10% sea water to the nutrient solution prevents trace element problems. It may be risky.

Chapter Seventeen
Novel Gardens

Many people who would like to grow their own think that they don't have the space. There are novel techniques that people can use to grow grass anywhere. Even people with only a closet, crawl space or just a shelf can grow their own.

The smallest space that can be used is a shelf 15–24 inches high. First, the space should be prepared as any other garden by making it reflective, using flat white paint, the dull side of aluminum foil, or white plastic. Fluorescents are the easiest and best way to illuminate the space. About twenty watts per square foot are used, or two tubes per foot of width. VHO fluorescents can be used to deliver more light to the system.

Plants can be started in 6 ounce cups or 8 to 16 ounce milk cartons placed in trays for easier handling.

With a shelf 3 feet or higher, plants can be grown in larger containers such as 4 or 6 inch pots, half gallon milk containers trimmed to hold only a quart.

The plants can be grown vertically only, as they normally grow, or moved to a horizontal position so that the main stem runs parallel to the light tubes. The plants' new growth will immediately face upwards toward the light. One gardener used an attic space only 4 feet tall. She let the plants grow until they reached 3 feet and and then turned them on their side. They used more floor space so she opened up a second bank of lights. At maturity, the plants were 3½ feet long and 2½ feet tall.

Another grower turned his basement with an 8 foot ceiling into a duplex growing chamber. Each unit had 3 foot tall plants.

If the plants are to be turned horizontally, then they are best grown in plastic bags or styrofoam cups so that they can be watered easily in their new positions. After being turned on the side, a hole is cut in the new top so the plants can be watered easily.

Some growers have wall space without much depth. This space can be converted to a growing area very easily. The space is painted white and a curtain is made so that the space is separated from the surrounding environment; this will keep light in and offers protection from nosey guests.

These plants were grown for a month on this 18 inch high shelf in 12 ounce styrofoam cups. Soon after this photo was taken, the plants were placed in a 36 inch shelf with overhead and side lighting.

These plants got too tall for the shelf so the styrofoam cups were turned horizontally. Holes were cut out of the side of the cups for easy watering.

Young plants on a low shelf.

The fluorescents should be placed so that they form a bank facing the plants. Although the plants naturally spread out, their depth or width can be controlled by training them using stakes or chicken wire placed on a frame. Wire or plastic netting is attached to the walls so that there is at least a 1 inch space between the wire and the wall. Some people build a frame out of 2 x 4's. Twist ties are used to hold the branches to the frame. Additional light can be supplied by placing a fluorescent unit on either end of the garden or along its length.

Growers who have a little more space for their garden, with a minimum width of 1 or 2 feet, can grow plants without training them. Fluorescent lights can be used to light the garden by hanging the light fixture from the top. All sides should be covered with reflective material. A metal halide lamp mounted on a movable apparatus will help the plants grow even faster so that the entire garden is illuminated several times during each light cycle.

Some people can spare only a small closet. Closets usually are designed in one of two shapes: square or long and rectangular. In any closet up to six feet long the simplest way to grow is by painting the inside of the closet white and hanging a metal halide light from the ceiling. Closets with dimensions of 5 x 5 or less need only a 400 watt metal halide although they can accomodate 1000 watt lamps. Larger areas need at least two 400 watt halide lamps.

Thin, rectangular closets are served best by a metal halide unit mounted on a solar shuttle type device. A fluorescent light unit hung from above the garden also works well. Additional fluorescent tubes can be used to supplement the top lights. It is convenient to mount them on either end of the hanging fixture if the closet is long enough so that they do not use potential growing space. A closet 2 feet by 7 feet might be illuminated by a 400 watt metal halide on a track, two 6 foot long VHOs or 4 regular fluorescent tubes hung from the ceiling. A grower might also use 14 screw-in 8 inch circular reflectors mounted on two 2 x 4s and hung above the garden. About 8 combination 8 and 12 inch circular fixtures will also light the area.

As the plants grow taller, fluorescent lit gardens will respond to fluorescent tubes placed on the sides of the garden below the tops of the plants. This light will help lower buds develop.

One of the main problems inherent in the nature of small gardens is the lack of ventilation and CO_2. For good growth rates the air should be enriched with CO_2 or provided with a fan for ventilation.

A garden in a closet.

Illustration by Rob M. Harper

is close up of a White Widow shows the glands which contain the T.H.C.

this canopy of a Sea of Green Garden, the entire space is covered with leaves.

This is a new seedling with cotyleon leafs emerging from the shell.

Soon the seedling grows its first true leaves. Eve this single blade has the characteristic cannabis sha and look.

This clone is being transplanted. The stem and root ball are held in place while soil is poured in the contair around them. *The stem is planted below its original surface.* Once the container is filled, the soil is patt down gently.

This young female plant is identified by the stigmas protruding from each ovary.

A more mature female plant can be identified by its denser flowers. In a few weeks they will develop into a compact bud.

This young male flower is identified by the distinctive ball shape of the flowers before they open.

Flowers on this male plant are beginning to open.

This aeroponic system is available commercially from several manufacturers. The container receives a constant spray of water and the roots grow down into the extremely moist air.

This is a two layered garden using the reserv method. The cuttings are grown underneath th flowering plants. This extremely easy to care f hydroponic system can be contained in a 4 foot x foot closet, as shown.

Powered by a fish tank air pump this recirculating constant drip system is easy to care for and produces excellent results. Each container is an independent system, is easy to move around, and can be bought at most garden stores.

The water nutrient solution feeding this plant essential for healthy growth.

This soil planting medium is easy to care for and produces a reliable crop. Soil is a very forgiving medium and despite the mistakes a grower may make, a good crop should be produced.

These are cuttings in a Rockwool system which will later be transplanted to a Rockwool slab. This system requires daily attention but can produce phenomenal growth rates. It can be easily assembled from parts available at Hardware and Gardening Stores.

An aeroponic system will produce vigorous roots like this. Water is constantly recirculated and sprayed over the roots.

The clones were rooted in Rockwool cubes and immediately forced into flowering. Shown here at maturity, the clones were less than a foot tall.

This unit is meant for plants which will grow several feet tall. Covering this Rockwool slab with white plastic, reflects light and prevents algae build up.

A simple drip system can be made to water the plants automatically. The water drips from the plants into a gutter, is recirculated to a reservoir, and then cycled back to the plants.

This recirculating N F T constant flow system was made from stock hardware and plumbing parts. The roots grow out of the cubes and stretch along the bottom of the tubes, which hold a shallow stream of water.

A typical meter long tray sold in European Grow Stores, but generally unavailable in the US, holds standard Rockwool, Coir, or PU Slab.

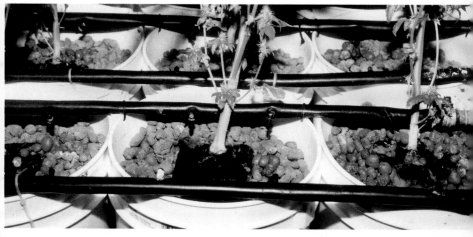

This home-made constant drip hydroponic system uses 2 gallon buckets. Rockwool cubes are used for cloning and then transferred to the hydro stone.

These larger plants are supported and shaped using wooden stakes. Twist ties hold the stem, to the supports and are also used to pull the branches inward.

Layering wide net over the garden allows the stems to grow through the net squares and immediately receive support.

These plants which would be ungainly if not controlled, are contained using chicken wire cages. Although some of the plants have long branches the wire prevents them from stretching into their neighbors' space.

ants in this garden were allowed to grow to 4 feet before they were forced to flower. These mostly Sativas
brids were 8 to 10 feet tall when they finished harvesting. Because most of the light was trapped in the
pper canopy the lower portions of the plant produced little yield.

is miniature forest is composed of clones that were forced to flower. They were spaced at approximately
per square foot and were less than a foot tall at harvest.

This plant is the victim of an extremely bad mite pest infestation. As population rises the mites start creating webs.

This is a leaf with a mite infestation. The mites u: their probuses to suck out plant juices and leavir tell tale dots.

Using incompatible fertilizers created severe potassium deficiency caused by lock up and precipitatic of the elements.

The plants seen on the right suffered from magnesium deficiency. When the plants on left were treated with magnesium sulfate, they showed recovery after 2 weeks.

This is what an aphid infestation looks like. The aphids, their nymphs, and discarded skins from molts are easily identifiable and congregate on the underside of the leaves.

The top of this leaf is showing necrotic spots where aphids have sucked out the leaves' juices.

This system originally designed for aeroponics was converted to a deep reservoir system. The pump pushe water through hoses located along the inside bottom of each large tube. Overflow water drains into th reservoir and eventually travels back to the pump.

Bottom left, an online CO2 monitoring unit keeps fraction of a second tabs on CO2 levels and opens or shuts a natural gas valve (not pictured) to a CO2 generator, pictured above.

In an automatic shading system within a larg greenhouse like this, plants can be forced t flower at any time. This long season variety w forced to flower during the summer using th shading technique.

WHITE WIDOW®: Female Brazilian x male Indian results in 60/40 sativa-indica ratio. Early forcing results in 18-25" plant, later forcing in 40" tall, bushy plant with short branches. Excellent for sea of green. Combination of body and cerebral high. High yields, flowering 75 days. Photo©Greenhouse Seed Co.

WHITE WIDOW PEACEMAKER®: A new hybrid in the white series. Early forcing results in a 20"-30" plant; later forcing results in a 40"-50" inch plant with strong upright branches. Intense taste and aroma with immediate body high. High yields; flowering 70 days. Photo©White Widow Master. Master Seed Co.

SHIVA SKUNK®: Skunk x Northern Lights #5. Early forcing results in 12"-15" plants; later 55" plants. Slight stretching and branching. Very resinous, pungent, and easy to grow. Like Skunk #1 with hybrid vigor results in larger buds. Moderate yields; flowering 60 days. Photo©Sensi Seeds

HAZE SKUNK®: Almost 100% sativa. Early forcing results in 18" plants; later forcing produces 60" plant with strong lateral branching. Best for garden with large plants and needs intense lighting. Extremely potent, mind altering haze high. Moderate yields; flowering 85 days. Photo©Dutch Passion.

SENSI STAR®: Mostly indica hybrid. Early forcing produces single a single 12" stem; later forcing a 40" plant. Short, controllable, lateral branches. Resinous, very compact buds with dense, sweet aroma and expanding smoke. Moderate-heavy yields; flowering 70 days. Photo©Paradise Seeds.

LEDO UNO®: Sativa predominant. Early forcing results in 12"-15" inch plants with little side branching; later forcing at 18" it reaches 60" with heavy lateral branching. Produces dense, long colas with heavy resin production . Moderate-heavy yields; flowering 70 days. Photo©K.C.Brains

STONEHEDGE®: California hybrid x Cambodian. Early forcing results in a 24" single stem plant, later forcing results in a 50" bushy plant. A short branched plant very suitable for sea of green. Both Cerebral and body high with a spicy taste and aromatic aftertaste. High yields; flowering 75 days. Photo©Sagarmatra Seeds

BIG TREAT®: Dutch Treat female x Big Skun results in dominant sativa. Early forcing results i 25-30" plant, later forcing in 60" plant. Cerebra high. High Yield, Flowering 75 days. Photo©Barge Spice of Life Seeds, c/o Hemp B.C.

Although some growers would consider this bud ready to harvest, it is really a week or two away. The potency of the glands will increase considerably as they fill with THC. Variety: Juicy Fruit.

In just a few days this bud's stigmas will dry and turn colored while the unfertilized ovaries behind them swell. The glands will stretch to a mushroom shape as they fill with THC.

This bud is ready to harvest, all but the top stigmas have turned brown and the glands have filled, covering the bud with a crystal formation. Variety: White Widow.

This is a close-up of a ripe bud ready to harvest.

After manicuring the fresh plant while it's hanging these growers will leave it to dry.

Both the fan leaves and outer leaves protecting the female flowers are removed, keeping only the flowers and very small leaves on the bud.

The Clipper, is the first semi-automatic clipping machine. It uses a rotating blade and a vacuum to manicure buds at 4 to 5 times the rate of a good manicurist. It requires easily learned technique and skill.

Chapter Eighteen
Containers

To save space, plants can be germinated in small containers and transplanted to progressively larger ones.

Seeds can be germinated in 2 X 1 inch trays or in peat pellets and remain in these containers for about one week.

Four inch diameter containers can hold the plants for 2 to 3 weeks without inhibiting growth.

Styrofoam cups weighted at the bottom with sand or gravel so they don't tip over are convenient germinating containers. If plants are to be germinated at one location and then moved to another location, styrofoam and other lightweight plastic cups are ideal containers.

Six ounce cups hold plants for about 7–10 days after germination. Sixteen ounce cups holds plants 10–20 days, as long as the plants receive frequent water replenishments.

Half gallon containers can support plants for 25–40 days.

Plants probably grow a bit faster without being transplanted. However, the saving in space for a multi-crop system or even a multi-light system more than compensates for the loss in growth rate. Figure that each transplanting costs the plants 3–4 days of growth. Growers using a 2 light system need to use only one lamp for the first 4–6 weeks the plants are growing. Multi-crop gardens need to use only a fraction of the space for the first 3 to 8 weeks after germination.

Some growers sex the plants before either the first or second transplanting. They find it easier to control the light-darkness cycle in a small space. Another crop's flowering cycle may coincide with the seedlings. To sex the small plants, only a small area is required in the grow room.

A good rule of thumb is that for each two feet of growth, a half gallon of growing medium is required in a garden in which fertilizers are supplied throughout the growing period. A 2 foot plant requires a ½ gallon container, a 5 foot plant uses a 2½ gallon container and a 10 foot plant requires a 5 gallon unit. Of course, plants' width or depth varies too, so these are approximations. Certainly there is no harm done in growing a plant in a container larger than is required. However, growing plants in containers which are too small delays growth or may even stunt the plants.

Plants growing in soil or compost-based mediums do better in slightly larger containers. A rule of thumb for them is a ¾ gallon medium for each foot of growth. A 5 foot plant requires a 3¾ gallon containers.

One grower wrote "I never use more than 4 gallon containers and have grown plants to 12 feet high with no signs of deficiencies. I was able to water at 2–3 day intervals. My 3 month old plants under light were in ½ gallon containers with and without wicks." This grower always uses small (½ gallon) containers for his spring greenhouse crop.

A plant growing in an organic-based medium such as soil-compost-manure and additives needs no fertilization if it is given a large enough container. For a five month growing season, plants in a rich mixture require 1 to 1½ gallons medium per foot. A 5 foot plant requires a container holding 5–7 ½ gallons.

Containers should have a slight graduation so that plants and medium can slide out easily.

Plastic containers or pots are the most convenient to use. They are lightweight, do not break and are inert. Metal containers react with the nutrients in the solution. Plastic bags are convenient containers. Grow bags have a square bottom so that they balance easily. However growers use all kinds of plastic bags for cultivation. Fiber containers are also popular. They are inexpensive, last several growing seasons and are easy to dispose of.

PART IV.
Planting

Chapter Nineteen
When to Plant

Marijuana growers using only artificial light can start at any time since the grower determines the plant's environment and stimulates seasonal variations by adjusting the light/darkness periods.

Gardeners using natural light either as a primary or secondary source must take the seasons into account. They plant in the spring — from April through June. These plants will be harvested between September and November and no artificial light may be needed as long as there is plenty of direct sunshine. Supplemental artificial light may help the plants to maturity in the fall, when the sun's intensity declines and there are overcast days. The angle of the sun's path changes over the season too. Areas may receive indirect sun during part of the growing season. In overcast areas, and even sunny places receiving direct sunlight, 4–6 hours of supplemental metal halide light during the brightest part of the day is all that is needed during September/October to help the buds mature. One lamp will cover about 100 square feet or an area 10 by 10 feet.

Growers using natural light are not restricted to one season. It is feasible to grow 3 or 4 crops a year using supplemental light. In early October, before the plants are harvested, seeds are started in a separate area. Since little room is needed for the first few weeks, they can be germinated on a shelf. In addition to natural light, the plants should get a minimum of 6 hours of artificial light per day at the rate of about 10 watts per square foot.

For fastest growth, the plants should receive 24 hours of light a day. Seedlings may receive light only during normal day light hours except that they require an interruption of the night cycle so they do not go into the flowering stage prematurely. If metal halide lamps are being used, a separate light system should be installed with incandescent or fluorescent lights on a timer so that the seedlings do not have a long period of uninterrupted darkness. One 60 watt incandescent bulb or one 22 watt fluorescent tube is used per square yard (3 by 3 feet). The bulbs can be flashed on for a few minutes using a multi-cycle timer during the middle of the dark period. Gardeners with large spaces sometimes stagger the timing of the night lights.

Incandescent bulbs are not very efficient, but they provide enough light to prevent flowering, they are easy and inexpensive to set up and maintain, and they light up almost immediately. In addition, they emit a high percentage of red light, which is part of the spectrum used by plants to regulate photoperiod responses. Metal halides require about 10 minutes to attain full brightness. Metal halide ballasts wear out faster when they are turned on and off a lot, so it is cheaper to flash incandescents.

In late December, the incandescents are turned off so that they no longer interrupt the night cycle. Within a week or two the plants will begin to flower. They will be ready to harvest in 6 or 8 weeks.

At the same time that the incandescents are turned off the winter crop, seeds are started for the spring crop. They are kept on the interrupted night regimen until late winter, around March 1-10. The plants will begin to flower and be ready in late May and early June. The spring crop should be planted with short season plants so that they do not revert back to vegetative growth as the days get longer. Long season varieties are more likely to revert.

After the flowers are formed, the spring crop plants will revert back to vegetative growth. New leaves will appear and the plant will show renewed vigor. The plant can be harvested again in the fall, or new seeds can be germinated for the fall crop.

One grower reported that he makes full use of his greenhouse. He starts his plants indoors in late November and starts the flowering cycle in the beginning of February. The plants are ripe by the end of April, then he lets the plants go back into vegetative growth for a month and a half. Then he starts to shade them again and harvests in late August. Next he puts out new, month-old, foot-high plants. He lets them grow under natural light, but breaks the darkness cycle using incandescent lights. In mid-September he shuts the lights off, and the plants mature in early November.

Chapter Twenty
Planting

Growers usually figure that ¼–⅓ of the seeds they plant reach maturity. Usually 40–50% of the plants are male. The best females are chosen for continued growth during early growth but after the plants have indicated.

Most fresh seeds have a very high germination rate, usually about 95%. However, older seeds (more than 2 or 3 years old) or seeds imported from foreign countries where they undergo stress during curing, may not fare so well. They have a higher percentage of weak plants and they are subject to disease. Sometimes virtually all of the seeds from a batch of imported marijuana are dead.

Intact seeds which are dark brown or grey have the best chance of germinating. Seeds which are whitish, light tan or cracked are probably not viable. Most guide books suggest that growers plant the largest seeds in a batch, but the size of the seed is genetically as well as environmentally determined and does not necessarily relate to its germination potential.

If the seeds are fresh, they can be planted one per container. They may be planted in the container in which they are to grow to maturity or in a smaller vessel. Some growers find it more convenient to plant the seeds in small containers to save space during early growth.

(A) A seedling pops out of the ground (B) and splits its shell. (C) Within a day the first set of true leaves emerge.

Seeds on the left have just popped their shell and are ready to plant. Germinated seeds on right can still be planted, but are really past their prime. Photo by T.L.

Healthy seedlings.

These plants were started in a primitive greenhouse constructed of tree branches and polyethylene film. It was only a foot and a half high. During the day the top was taken off. Towards the evening, the plastic tops were replaced. To prevent freezing, an extra layer of plastic was placed over the garden and filled plastic water jugs which heated up during the day radiated heat at night.

Seeds with a dubious chance of germination are best started in tissue and then placed in pots as they show signs of life. The wet tissue, napkin or sponge is placed in a container or on a plate, and is covered with plastic wrap. The seeds are checked every 12 hours for germination. As soon as the root cracks the skin, the seedling is planted with the emerging point down. Seeds can also be started in tray pots so that large numbers can be tried without using much space.

Seedlings and cuttings can be placed in the refrigerator — not the freezer — to slow down their growth if it is inconvenient to plant at the moment. They can be stored in the vegetable crisper of the refrigerator for a week or more, in a moistened plastic bag. The temperature should be kept above 40 degrees to prevent cell damage. This does not adversely affect the plant's later growth, and in fact, is an easy way to harden the plants up that are placed outdoors later.

Seeds should be sown ¼–½ inch deep, covered, and then the medium should be patted down. Seeds sown in light soil or planting mixes can be sown one inch deep. Some growers treat the seeds with B_1 or the rooting hormone, indolebutyric acid, which is sold as an ingredient in many rooting solutions. Seeds germinated in covered trays or mini-greenhouses grow long, spindly stems unless the top is removed as the first seedlings pop the soil. The medium must be kept moist.

One way to make sure that the medium remains moist is to plant the seeds in containers or nursery trays which have been modified to use the wick system. To modify a tray, nylon cord is run horizontally through holes in each of the small growing spaces. The cord should extend downward into a leakproof holder. (Trays come with 2 kinds of holders. Some have drainage holes and some are solid.) The tray is raised from the holder using a couple of pieces of 2 x 4's running lengthwise which keep tray holders filled with water. The tray will remain moist as long as there is water in the bottom. If the tray is to be moved, it is placed in a cardboard box or over a piece of plywood before being filled with water.

The light is kept on continuously until the seeds germinate. Most seeds germinate in 3–14 days. Usually fresh seeds germinate faster than old ones.

Chapter Twenty–One
Early Growth

Once the seeds germinate, the light is kept on for 18–24 hours a day. Some growers think that there is no significant difference in growth rates between plants growing under 24 hours of light a day (continuous lighting) and those growing under an 18 hour light regimen. In controlled experiments there was a significant difference: the plants get off to a faster start given continuous lighting. Some growers cut the light schedule down to conserve electricity.

Plants grown under continuous light which are moved outdoors occasionally experience shock. This may be caused by the intense light they receive from the sun combined with the shortened day length.

Another popular lighting regimen starts with continuous light. A week after germination the light is cut back one hour so that the regimen consists of 23 hours on and one hour off. The following week the lights are cut back again, to 22 hours of light and 2 of darkness. Each week thereafter, the lights are cut back another hour until the light is on only 12 hours a day.

Whenever a light is to be turned on and off periodically, it is best to use a timer to regulate it. The timer is never late, always remembers, and never goes on vacation.

Plants are at their most vulnerable stage immediately after they germinate. They are susceptible to stem rot, which is usually a fungal infection and occurs frequently when the medium is too moist and the roots do not have access to oxygen. On the other hand, if the medium dries out, the plant may be damaged from dehydration.

Mice, pet birds, dogs and cats have all been noted to have a fondness for marijuana sprouts and the young plants.

Seedlings given too little light or too warm an environment stretch their stems. The long slender shoot subsequently has problems staying upright — it becomes top-heavy. These plants should be supported using cotton swabs, toothpicks or thin bamboo stakes.

Most seedlings survive the pitfalls and within a matter of weeks develop from seedlings into vigorous young plants. During marijuana's early growth, the plant needs little special care. It will have adjusted to its environment and grow at the fastest pace the limiting factors allow.

If the plants are in a soilless mix without additives they should be fertilized as soon as they germinate. Plants grown in large containers with soil or a mix with nutrients can usually go for several weeks to a month with no supplements.

Within a few weeks the plants grow quite a bit and gardeners thin the plants. If possible, this is not done until the plants indicate sex, so that the grower has a better idea of how many plants to eliminate. The most vigorous, healthy plants are chosen.

Fluorescent grown seedlings fell over when they were transported to the greenhouse. They were transplanted deeply so that their stems did not need to be staked.

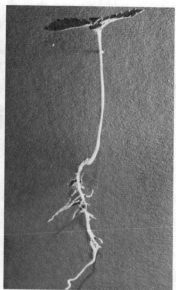

These seedlings stretched due to inadequate light.

Seedling with well developed root system. Photo by T.L.

(A) Seedling is held in place as the soil is added to the pot. (B) Transplanting completed.

A few weeks after transplanting.

A month after the first transplanting the plants were repotted. This photo was taken 1 week later.

Chapter Twenty–Two
Watering

Growers using passive hydroponic systems only have to water by adding it to the reservoirs, to replenish water lost to evaporation and transpiration.

Growers using active hydroponic systems, including drip emitters, adjust the watering cycle so that the medium never loses its moisture. Mediums for active systems are drained well so that the roots come into contact with air. Each medium retains a different volume of water. The plant's size and growth stage, the temperature, and the humidity also affect the amount of water used. Cycles might start at once every six hours of light during the early stages and increase as the plants require it.

Plants growing in soil or soilless mixes should be watered before the soil dries out but only after the top layer has lost a bit of its moisture. If the mixture is not soggy and drains well, overwatering is not a problem. Excess moisture drains.

Plants have problems with some soils not because they are too wet, but because the soils have too fine a texture and do not hold air in pockets between the particles. As long as a medium allows both air and water to penetrate, the roots will remain healthy. If the roots do not have access to air, they grow weak and are attacked by bacteria.

Plant leaves catch dust so it is a good idea to spray the plants every 2–4 weeks with a fine spray, letting the water drip off the leaves. Do this before the beginning of the light cycle so the leaves dry off completely, and the glass of the lights is not hot in case water touches it.

Some growers spray the leaves weekly with a dilute fertilizer solution. The leaf has pores through which the nutrients can be absorbed and utilized. They claim that the growth rate is increased. In various tests with legal plants, researchers have affirmed that plants which are foliar-fed do grow faster.

Once the flowers start forming, the plants should not be sprayed because the flowers are susceptible to mold and infections which are promoted by excess humidity.

Chapter Twenty–Three
Pruning

There are probably more theories about pruning and its effect on crop yield as there are cultivators. Pruning theories are complicated by the many varieties of marijuana, which have different branching patterns and growing habits.

Indicas tend to grow naturally with little branching. Most of their energy is used for the central main bud which may develop to a diameter of 3 to 4 inches. Branches are short and compact.

Mexicans, Colombians, and Africans usually grow in a conical pattern often likened to a Christmas tree. They develop a large central bud. The peripheral buds and branches can also grow quite large.

Plants regulate their growth patterns using auxins, which are hormones. One auxin is produced by the tallest growing tip of the plant. This inhibits other branches from growing as fast. If the top bud is removed, the two branches below grow larger, in effect becoming the main stem. They produce the growth-inhibiting auxin; however, they have less of an inhibitory effect on the lower branches.

Growers are often obsessed with the yield per plant. This outlook developed because of the surreptitious nature of marijuana cultivation. Farmers and gardeners can grow only a few plants so they want to get the best possible yield from them. Traditional farmers are more concerned with the yield per unit of space. Since indoor gardeners have a limited space, total yield of high quality marijuana should be of more concern than the yield per plant.

Growers have done experiments showing that some pruning techniques effectively increase the yield of some plants. However, the pruned plants usually occupy more space than plants which are left unpruned, so that there may be no increase in yield per unit of space.

To make a plant bushy it is pinched (the growing shoot is removed) at the second or third set of leaves and again at the sixth, seventh or eighth internode. Sometimes the plants are pinched once or twice more. This encourages the plants to spread out rather than to grow vertically.

Plant branching can be controlled by bending instead of cutting. If the top branch is bent so that it is lower than the side branches, the side shoots will start to grow as if the top branch was cut because the branch highest from the ground produces the growth auxin. If the top branch is released so that it can grow upward again it starts to dominate again, but the side branches still have more growth than they ordinarily would have had. Top branches can also be "trained" to grow horizontally so that the primary bud is exposed to more light. The bud will grow larger than normal. Bamboo stakes, twist-ties and wire can be used for training.

One grower trained his plants using a technique ordinarily used by grape growers. He built a frame made of a single vertical 2 x 3 and nailed 4 foot long 2 x 1's every 9 inches along its length so that the horizontal boards stretched 2 feet in either direction. Then he trained the branches to the frame. Each branch was stretched horizontally and the plant had virtually no depth. This increased the number of plants he could grow since each plant took less space.

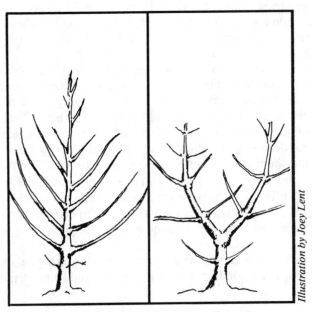

Illustration by Joey Lent

When center of the plant is cut, there is more side branching.

On the next crop he used the same system with most of his plants but set up a chickenwire fence on a frame about 6 inches from one wall. As the plants grew he trained them to the fence.

A grower in Mendocino pinches the plants at the fourth node and then allows only four branches to develop. She removes all side shoots. Each plant grows four giant buds and takes relatively little space.

Plants which are only a foot or two tall when they were put into the flowering cycle may not have developed extensive branching. They may grow into plants with only one bud; the main stem becomes swollen with flowers but there is little branching. These plants require only about a square foot of floor space. Although their individual yields are low, the plants have a good yield-per-space unit. A gardener with larger plants modified this technique by trimming off all side shoots and spacing the one-buds close together to maximize yield.

A greenhouse grower grew plants to about three feet and then clipped the tops. Each plant developed four top stems in a couple of weeks. Then he turned the light cycle down to induce flowering.

Illustration by Joey Lent

A bushy regrowth plant and a trained plant.

A garden in the midwest featured plants which were trained to 5 foot tomato trellises (the metal cones). The grower trained the branches around the cone and tied them to the support using twist-ties.

Plants which are several feet tall can also be turned on their sides as was discussed in the chapter on Novel Gardens. The plant immediately switches its growth pattern so that the stems grow vertically, against the gravity and towards the light.

Most growers agree that plants should not be clipped once they are in a pre-flowering stage. By experience they know that this may seriously decrease yield.

Plants may grow at an uneven pace in the garden. There are several reasons for this. The plants may differ genetically and be inclined to grow at different rates, or there may be an uneven distribution of light in the garden so that some plants receive more energy to fuel their growth. Plants in single containers can be moved around the garden to even out the amount of light they get and to deal with the problem of height. When the taller plants are placed at the periphery of the garden, light is not blocked from the shorter ones. Taller plants need not be clipped. Instead, their tops can be bent and snapped so that the stem is horizontal near the top. This technique is used as far as 2 feet below the top of the stem. The bent tops usually need to be supported. It is not hard to tie one end of a bamboo stake to the main stem and the other end to the top, so that a triangle is formed.

Contrary to myth, sun leaves should not be removed from the plant except late in life when they often yellow. These leaves are little sugar factories which turn the light energy into chemical energy which is stored and used later. When the leaf is removed, the plant loses a source of energy and its rate of growth slows. If you don't believe this, try an experiment. Find any type of plant which has two sun leaves opposite each other with a small branch growing from either side. Remove one of the leaves and see which side branch develops faster.

Chapter Twenty–Four
Pests

When plants are grown outdoors, pests and insects are ever-present but most of the time they are kept in check by the forces of nature. The wind, rain, changes in temperature, predators and diseases work as a system of checks and balances to keep the populations down despite a phenomenally high theoretical reproductive capacity.

Indoors, invading plant pests discover an ideal environment, with few of the hazards they would find outdoors and with an abundance of food. Within a few weeks of invasion the implications of the pest's theoretical multiplication rate are evident and the plants may suffer the ravages of the attack. For this reason, any pest invasion is treated very seriously and quickly.

Every insect invasion to the garden has a cause. Most of the time, the pests were carried into the garden by the gardener. Less frequently, pests enter through the windows, cracks, or through the ventilation system. Cautious growers never go into the indoor garden after working outdoors or being in an outdoor garden. They never work on healthy plants after being around or working on infected ones. In some commercial greenhouses, workers change clothing in a dressing room before entering from outside.

One grower keeps a plastic dishpan filled with salt water at the entrance to his grow room. As he enters the room he dips the soles of each shoe in the water. This kills any pests which might be riding on the undersides of his shoes.

To get a close look at insects, it is a good idea to get a photographer's loop magnifying glass or a portable low-power microscope. Even the most inexpensive ones are adequate.

There are six pests that are most likely to attack marijuana indoors: aphids, mealybugs, mites, whiteflies, scale, and caterpillars. A few others sometimes invade greenhouses. These include caterpillars, cutworms, grasshoppers and leafhoppers.

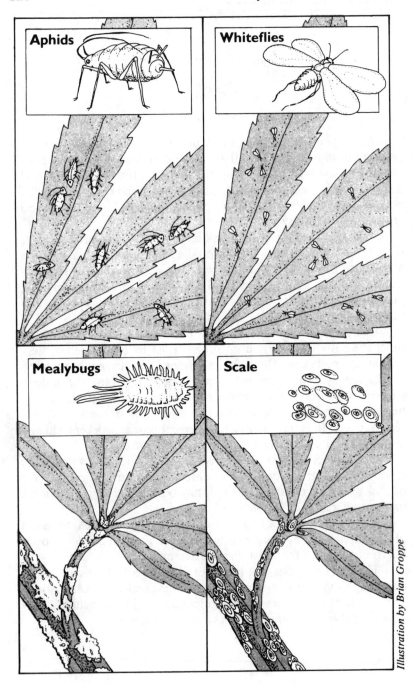

Aphids

Whiteflies

Mealybugs

Scale

Illustration by Brian Groppe

APHIDS

Aphids are usually found on the undersides of leaves and on stems, though they are sometimes found on the leaf tops. The adults are about $\frac{1}{32}$ to $\frac{1}{16}$ of an inch long and are oval, almost egg-shaped. They have two protrusions from their rear which look like pipes and may or may not have wings. They are usually found in dense colonies with an adult surrounded by a cluster of young. They are usually pale green or yellow, but sometimes are brown, black or red. They molt leaving a white shell. They secrete "honeydew" which is shiny and sticky and is found on infested foliage. Honeydew is a concentrate of the sugars the animal has sucked out of the plant and discarded in its search for protein. Aphids are frequently found together with ants which farm them for their honeydew by carrying them from plant to plant.

Infested plants weaken from the insects' constant sucking of sap which they eat by penetrating the deep tissue. Older leaves curl and younger ones grow deformed. Mold sometimes forms on the honeydew. Within weeks the plant may wither. Aphids are carriers of molds and viruses.

Indoors, aphids reproduce parthenogenetically; that is, all the insects are females and they can reproduce without being fertilized. They bear live young, which may actually carry embryos of their own before they are born. They can reproduce when they are 6 days old.

Luckily, aphids are not difficult to control. Action is taken at the first sign of infection. First, the garden is checked for ants. Any colonies are eliminated using ant bait, ant stakes or boric acid.

Then all visible aphids are wiped off the plants using a sponge and soapy water, a soapy water spray or insecticide. A soapy water spray is made by mixing 1½ tablespoons Ivory Snow Flakes® or any other soap without detergent in a gallon of water. Some growers reported success using Dr. Bronner's Eucalyptus or Mint liquid soaps® (these are often found in health food stores) at the rate of 1 tablespoon per gallon. This will eliminate most of the pests so that the grower has some breathing space. However, even the most thorough spraying or sponging does not eliminate all of the pests, and since they reproduce parthenogenetically, even one remaining insect can restart the colony.

If the plants are not flowering, then spray can be used every 2 or 3 days for several weeks. Thorough sprayings may eventually destroy the colony. They certainly keep it in check.

Another convenient spray is available commercially. Pyrethrum is a natural insecticide found in chrysanthemum-family plants. It has not been found harmful to warm-blooded animals but is toxic to aphids, among other insects. Pyrethrum may be purchased as a powder, a liquid concentrate, in a pump or aerosal spray. Usually growers with small gardens choose the aerosols for convenience, while those with large gardens find the concentrates or powders much less expensive.

Some benign insects like to eat aphids and are convenient to use in a greenhouse or grow-room situation. Ladybugs and green lacewings are predators which eat aphids. They can be purchased commercially from insectiaries. These insects also go through a rapid lifecycle and may eat hundreds of aphids as they grow to adults. The insects come with instructions for their use.

People are sometimes a little queasy about bringing beneficial insects indoors because they are afraid they will escape into unwanted areas. However, for the most part these insects stay where they belong as long as there is food for them to eat. Adult beneficials sometimes fly directly into metal halide lamps and die instantly. One grower placed a glass reflector around his lamps. The trick is to get the adult beneficials to lay eggs because the predators are most voracious during their immature stages. Given enough food (aphids) this presents no problem. Once the predators become established they keep the pest population at a negligible level, but never eliminate their source of food.

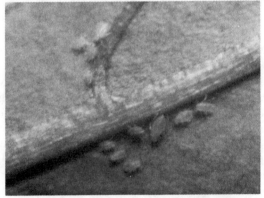

Aphids on a leaf. The mother can be seen with offspring.

MEALYBUGS

Mealybugs are light-colored insects which exude a white, waxy cottony-looking substance in which they nestle or which covers their body. They are usually found on the underside of the leaves and in the joints between the leaves and stems. The adults are from $\frac{1}{16}$ to $\frac{1}{8}$ inch long. They suck juices from the plant and exude honeydew. Their breeding rate is much slower than many other pests; a generation takes a month or more.

A small mealybug infection may be eliminated by using a sponge to wipe the creatures off the plants. They can also be destroyed using a cotton swab dabbed in alcohol, which kills them instantly. More serious infestations may be controlled using a soapy water solution or pyrethrum. As well as eating aphids, green lacewings also eat mealybugs.

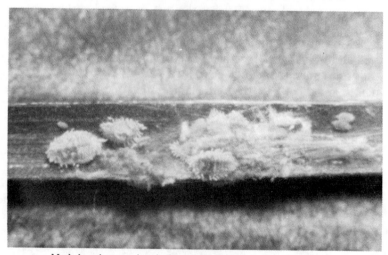

Mealy bugs hang out in colonies and produce a cottony looking wax.

MITES

Mites are the most damaging pest that can enter a garden. They are not insects, but an arachnid, which is the class of animals that include spiders. Mites are tiny and may not be noticed until they have developed into a serious infestation. There are many species of mites. However the one most likely to attack the garden is the 2 spotted mite, which has two spots on its back which can be seen under a magnifying glass.

The first indication that a grower may have mites is seeing pinpoint yellow spots on fan leaves. These spots are located above the points where the mites have pierced the tissue to suck out the plant juices. Mites are very small, measuring only 3–6 thousandths of an inch. They look like small dots colored black, red or brown. Mites' maturity and reproductive rates are affected by temperature. A female lays about 100 eggs during her lifetime, but at 60 degrees she produces 20 offspring, at 70 degrees she and her offspring number 13,000, and at 80 degrees she represents a potential 13,000,000 individuals over a single month. Under ideal conditions mites reproduce a week after hatching.

As the mite population rises, the plants weaken. Infested leaves curl under and spider-like webbing is spun which covers the plants and is used by the pests to move from plant to plant. Mites also walk down stems, across medium and across dry space in search of new plants to colonize. Besides the leaf spots and curling, infested leaves sometimes also bronze and/or develop necrotic brown spots.

Most growers do not notice mites until the infestation has been well established and there has been damage to plants. The situation calls for immediate action. First, after careful examination, infested plants are separated from the uninfested ones. Lightly infested plants may be separated from heavily damaged plants. (Physical barriers such as sticky tape are placed around the heavily infested plants, pots or the garden perimeter to prevent migration of mites. Tops are separated so that the mites cannot walk from plant to plant via foliage.)

Mites suck juices, so they must evaporate large quantities of water. This is easier for them to do in a dry environment. Humid environments slow down their metabolism, life span, and reproductive rate.

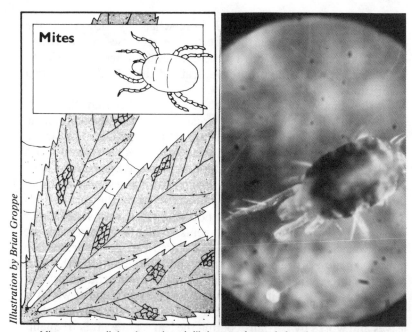

Illustration by Brian Groppe

Mites are so small that the gardener is likely to see damage before the pests are detected.
Photo by T. L.

As the mite population increases, they spin webs for easy transport. Photo by T.L.

Mites may be controlled somewhat by lowering the temperature, thus slowing the insects' life processes considerably. Even if this is done only during the dark cycle, when it is easier to lower temperatures, the progression rate of the infection is slowed significantly.

Mites tend to congregate on the leaves rather than the buds, although, as their populations increase, they can start colonizing the buds as well. They can be washed off the leaves using a strong water spray. Growers sometimes use a soapy water spray from a small gauge directional nozzle. Medium pressure can be used. The floor and container surfaces are covered with newspaper or other throwaways so that the mites can be removed by the spray. Buds within 2 weeks of harvest should not be sprayed with soap. Other possible sprays include wetting agents, which interfere with the mites' water-holding ability, flour or starch (½ cup flour, ½ cup milk in a gallon of water) which trap and kill the mites as the mixture dries into a thin film, and an anti-transpiration product, "Wilt-Pruf"® which is sold in many nurseries. It is a chemical which is used to slow down the rate at which plants lose water through their leaves and works by partially coating the leaf's pores. It is frequently used when transplanting and during dry, hot, or sunny periods. Wilt-Pruf also traps mites in its thin film. When these products are used, individual leaves are sprayed using a hand trigger bottle.

Some growers "homebrew" a miticide using common spices such as garlic, cayenne pepper, onion, cloves or their combinations soaked in water. Recipes call for either grinding the raw spices or boiling them. One gallon of water is mixed with one or more of the following: ½–1 ounce garlic, 2–3 ounces of onion, ½ ounce cloves, ½–1 ounce cayenne pepper. Before spraying all the plants with a homebrew, try it on a few leaves to make sure that the plants are not adversely affected and the mites are killed.

Insectiaries advertise predatory mites for the control of mites. There are several varieties that attack two-spotted mites. Choice of variety of predator mites depends on greenhouse temperature. Some growers have reported great success using these predators, while others report that they have been unsuccessful at getting them to take. When they get established they are effective, but sometimes they seem to disappear in the marijuana garden never to be seen again. Meanwhile, the mites continue to multiply at a geometric rate.

On May 23rd, 1986, the New York Times reported on Kelthane, the popular miticide and insecticide. Growers have often reported its effectiveness in eliminating pest problems. However, it turns out that one of the reasons for its effectiveness is that it contains DDT. You say that can't be: DDT was banned from use in 1972. Rohm & Haas Company of Philadelphia, which distributes the product manufactured overseas, has agreed to reduce the level in this product from 2.5% to $\frac{1}{10}$th of 1 percent on December 31, 1988. Yes, that's right, 1988. The stocks will be in stores well after that date. DDT damages the reproductive systems and nervous systems of mammals. For your own sake, please don't use Kelthane or any other miticide-insecticide-containing dicofol.

Since mites have a short regeneration cycle, for sprays to be effective they must be used often enough to kill each new generation before it has a chance to reproduce. To prevent buildup of resistance, different sprays are alternated. Several growers have reported eliminating mites using "Holiday Foggers" 3 times a day at 5 day intervals.

Smart growers cover their bodies and wear respirators when working with harmful chemicals. Exposed clothing and underwear is removed immediately after the operation is ended and is washed separately or disposed of. One grower used disposable paper jump suits he found at an army surplus store. Another used clothing one step away from the garbage. After removing clothing, the exposed individual showers well with strong soap.

Mites are difficult to eliminate or even control, but it can be done. The means of control depends upon the stage of the plants' life cycle and the degree of infestation. Gardens with a minor infection which are near harvest may be protected simply by lowering the temperature, or by using a quick knockdown spray.

Growers sometimes find it more convenient to destroy young plants with a mite infection than to try to combat it. Plants which are nearing the end of the vegetative stage may never flower well if the infection is severe, so that growers try to keep the population down on plants older than 2 months. Growers sometimes start the flowering cycle early when they detect mites. That way temperatures are lowered because of the longer darkness cycle, and the mites do not have as long to build up their population.

WHITEFLIES

Whiteflies look like flies except that they are all white. The adults are about $\frac{1}{16}$th of an inch long. They can be seen flying off foliage when it is shaken. They lay large white eggs which can be seen on the undersides of the leaves they inhabit. They suck sap from the leaves and leave spots of honeydew. Whiteflies spread black soot, molds and other diseases.

Whiteflies undergo four stages of development once they hatch from eggs. Each stage is called an instar. Their life cycle is strictly regulated by temperature. As temperatures increase from 55 to 85 degrees the number of days from egg to adult decreases from 103 to 18 days. However, the adult's life span also decreases. At 55 degrees, the adult lives over 60 days. At 85 degrees it lives fewer than 7 days. At 65 degrees it produces more than 300 eggs over its lifespan, at the rate of more than 8 eggs per day. As the temperature increases, total egg production decreases to less than 30 and the rate of production goes down to fewer than 5 per day.

The whitefly population must increase to tremendous numbers before there is any apparent damage to plants directly. However, the honeydew dropped by whiteflies becomes an incubation spot for mold.

Whiteflies are easy to control. If there only seem to be a few, they can be pinched off the leaves by hand. Their metabolism is a factor of temperature; at cool temperatures in the low 60's, they are sluggish and easily trapped. They are susceptible to spice sprays and

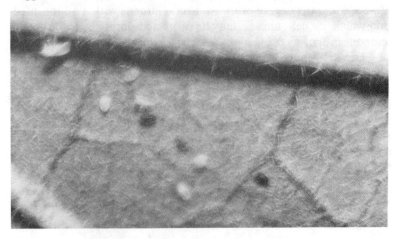

pyrethrum, but the easiest way to deal with them is using Encarsia Formosa, the whitefly parasite. This small non-social wasp is about ⅟₃₂nd of an inch long, about the same size as a mite. It lives entirely on whiteflies. The adults eat the eggs and the first and second instar. They lay their eggs in the third instar. As the wasp embryo develops in the whitefly instar, the egg, which was a pale green or tan, turns black. Encarsia formosa development is also regulated by temperature. At 55 degrees it takes 30 days to reach adulthood, but at 85 degrees it requires only about 10 days. At 65 degrees the adults live about 30 days, but only 8 days at 80 degrees. However the number of eggs laid by females, about 30, does not vary much. They just lay them over a shorter period of time.

Insectiaries usually suggest that whitefly parasites be released several times over a 3 week period allowing several generations of whitefly instars to be parasitized, assuring control of the problem quickly. However, experienced growers have found that only 1 release is required, although control takes a while longer. By the third generation the parasites achieve virtual control of the plant eaters and while they do not eliminate them, they keep the whiteflies down to a negligible level and prevent large outbreaks from occurring.

Whiteflies are attracted to certain shades of yellow. Nurseries sell cards which are either pre-glued or which can be coated with oil. Any whiteflies which fly to the card are trapped.

One grower uses a vacuum cleaner to collect whiteflies from his plants. He says that it is best to do this early in the morning when it is still cool and the insects are sluggish. He says that the vacuum is also effective against aphids.

SCALE

Scale are insects which attack the stems and undersides of leaves. There are two kinds of scale: armored and soft-bodied. Armored scale are ⅙–⅟₁₂ inch long and are usually brown, grey or reddish. They secrete a waxy or cottony substance which shapes a shell to protect their bodies. Soft-bodied scale are usually brown, black or mottled. Their skin is smooth and shiny. Both types are mobile only when they are young. Usually they lose their legs after the first or second moult. The males regain their legs as well as wings at the final moult and spend their short adult life in search of females to inseminate.

Scale females can produce up to 5,000 offspring over a lifetime, but they have a relatively slow rate of growth so that it takes a while for them to build a large population.

Scale suck sap, leaving little residue. Sometimes immature scale, which are mobile, excrete honeydew. Their saliva may be toxic to the plant. Leaves or branches will turn yellow and die.

Scale often look like nodes or blemishes on a stem. They are easily scraped off the plant using fingernails.

They do not often attack marijuana; however, some cases have been reported.

There are number of effective methods of controlling scale. Since they reproduce slowly, scraping the adults off the leaves and stems may be an effective control. Garlic-cayenne sprays may eliminate them. Finally, there are a number of parasites which attack the insects in their immature stages. Predators are often specific to a particular variety of scale, so it's best to send samples of the infection to insectiaries when buying them.

Scale can also be killed using a cotton swab dipped in alcohol.

CATERPILLARS

Caterpillars are a threat to all gardens. A single moth or butterfly can lay hundreds of eggs, and caterpillars have an enormous appetite. They can devastate a garden of sprouts overnight and can inflict severe damage to mature plants. Species vary as to tastes and habits. Some just munch on the leaves or buds, while others bore into the stems and eat out the plant's stem.

The caterpillars which remain on the surface are the easiest to locate and destroy. Once a caterpillar has burrowed into the plant it can be very difficult to find. Sometimes they can be located by looking for the characteristic burrowing hole at its usual location.

There are several ways to eliminate caterpillars. Handpicking can be very effective in a small garden. There are several natural insecticides which seem to be harmless to warm-blooded animals and which are lethal to these chewing pests. Bacillus thurengensis (BT) is a bacteria which causes plague in caterpillars. It is available commercially as a powder or spray and can eliminate pests within days. It remains effective until washed away by water. Pyrethrum is also effective against caterpillars. This insecticide is derived from the pyrethrum plant, a relative of the chrysanthemum.

When caterpillars have already burrowed into the stem, they must be sought out and destroyed or they will kill the plant. Some growers try to locate the burrow holes and then use a wire or flexible tool to squash the insect in its path. The stems can also be split with a sharp, clean knife or razor and then after the pest is killed the stem is sealed with grafting wax and bound with tape and reinforced with a brace.

Chapter Twenty–Five
Flowering

Earlier in the book (Chapter 3), we described how marijuana determines when it should flower. It senses the onset of "Fall" by measuring the number of hours of uninterrupted darkness. When the plant senses a period of uninterrupted darkness long enough each evening, it triggers into flowering.

The period of darkness required varies by variety. Equatorial varieties need a longer period of darkness than indica or Southern African varieties because the equatorial growing season is longer and equatorial plants have shorter days. Equatorial sativas flower when the dark cycle increases to 12 hours or more. Most indicas flower at between 12 to 16 hours of light, 8 to 12 hours of uninterrupted darkness.

Male marijuana plants flower before the females and are only partially light-sensitive. In some varieties the males seem to flower after a few months of growth, regardless of lighting conditions.

Since female marijuana flowering is regulated by light, a cultivator growing under lights can put the garden into flowering with the flick of the timer. Once the plants start to bloom, they will grow another foot or two in height. The plants should be set into flowering before they get too tall.

Growers use several lighting regimens to start the plants flowering. Growers using continuous light or another long day cycle can cut the light back to flowering cycle with no intermediate steps. The plants do not suffer from shock or exhibit unusual growth. Some growers do introduce the cycle more gently, cutting the light back to flowering cycle over several weeks.

After 4 to 5 weeks of heavy flowering, some growers set the light back another hour to simulate the shortening season. Growers cut the light back another hour after another month. This may be especially helpful in finishing some tropical varieties, which do not reach maturity in their native lands until the middle of the short day season (there is no winter in the tropics).

Black plastic was placed over
the garden each evening to
force flowering out of season.

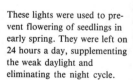

They were removed each morning. The plants received only 12 hours of light and continued to flower into early June when they were picked.

These lights were used to prevent flowering of seedlings in early spring. They were left on 24 hours a day, supplementing the weak daylight and eliminating the night cycle.

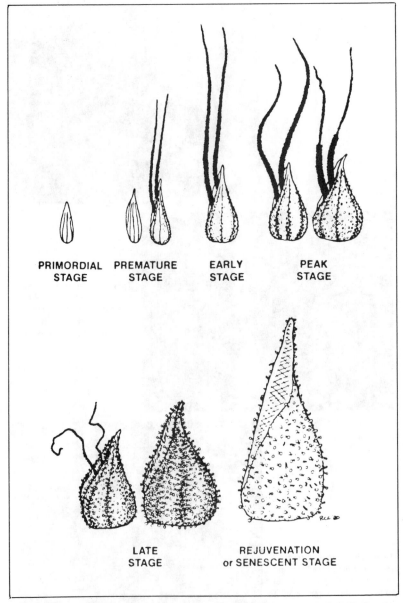

PRIMORDIAL   PREMATURE   EARLY   PEAK
STAGE   STAGE   STAGE   STAGE

LATE   REJUVENATION
STAGE   or SENESCENT STAGE

"Development of unfertilized calyx. Primordia develop pistils which wither and die as the calyx swells and resin production increases." R.C. Clarke. From MARIJUANA BOTANY © 1981 by R.C. Clarke, published by And/Or Press, Inc.

Chapter Twenty–Six
Sinsemilla and Sexing

The word "sinsemilla" is derived from the two Spanish words "sin" and "semilla" meaning respectively "without" and "seed". Connoisseurs prize sinsemilla partly because the marijuana has a greater potency and a more intense aroma than seeded marijuana, and partly because of its enhanced appearance.

In order for the flowers to ripen unseeded, they must remain unpollinated (unfertilized). Male and female flowers usually appear on separate plants. The males are removed from the space as soon as they are recognized. This should be done early in the male plants' development, before any large flower clusters appear. Even a single open flower cluster can release enough pollen to fertilize thousands of female flowers.

Males can be detected early by carefully examining the space where the leaf joins the stem (internode). Before the plant begins to develop flower clusters, a single male or female flower will sometimes grow in the internode. A male flower will have what looks like a bulb growing from a thin stem, and at the bulb's end there will be a curved protrusion that looks something like a little bent finger. A female flower will usually have two antennae-like protrusions jutting out. Sometimes a sexually indistinguishable flower appears.

Male flowers protrude from joints of young plants.

Male flowers develop quickly on elongating stem.

Male and female flowers. Photo courtesy *Hydro-King*, LaGrande, Oregon.

The females' leaves begin to grow closer together, forming a strong stem which will hold the clusters of flowers and later the ripening seed.

Any plants which have not indicated are watched closely, and the females are watched for any signs of hermaphrodites. These plants are primarily female but they produce some fertile male flowers. This may consist of only a few clusters, an entire branch or, occasionally, males throughout the plant. These plants are dangerous in any sinsemilla garden. Even a small cluster of flowers can ruin entire colas of buds. Either the male flowers should be removed and the plant checked daily, or the plant should be removed from the garden, which is the safest course of action.

There are several methods used to sex plants early. Since marijuana flowering is regulated by the number of hours of uninterrupted darkness, it is easy to manipulate the plant's flowering cycle. Young plants can be forced to indicate by putting them under a long night regimen. The plants will begin to indicate within a few days and after 10 days, fast growing plants should have clearly defined flowers. Once the plants indicate, the males can be separated from the females, and the garden can be returned to the vegetative growth cycle simply by changing the light regimen back to the long day/short night.

A few flowers are sometimes detected along joints of preflowering plants. These are females.

Development of young female flowers.

Putting the plants through an abbreviated flowering cycle sets them back several weeks. First, their growth is stopped and then it takes them some time to start growing again. Some growers feel that the plants lose a bit of vigor in the process. To eliminate stresses in the garden, a clone can be taken of each plant.

The clones should be tagged to denote plant of origin and then placed in water or rooting medium under a long night/short day environment. The clones will have the same sex as its clone parent, so the clone parent's sex is determined before the plant is out of the vegetative stage. The female clones can be continued under the flowering regimen and will provide a taste of the clone-parent's future buds.

Within a few days of the change in the light regimen to a long night, the plants begin to show changes in their growth patterns. First, their rate of growth, which might be as much as 2 inches a day during the previous cycle, slows and stops. Next the plants begin to differentiate. The males elongate upon ripening so that their flower sacks, which contain copious amounts of pollen, tower above the females. Marijuana is normally wind-pollinated.

The females start to grow stocky stems with shorter nodes between the leaves. The number of fingers on the leaves decreases and the plant may revert from opposite leaves to a pattern of leaves alternating on the stem.

Within a few weeks, large numbers of pistils (the white antennae) will form along the stem and on the tops of the branches. If the flowers are fertilized, the pistils will start to dry up, beginning at the tips. Each fertilized flower produces a seed. Such formation, which commences upon fertilization, is apparent by the third day. The ovary at the base of the pistil swells as the new seed grows inside of it.

As long as most flowers remain unfertilized, the plant continues to produce new flowers. The clusters get thick with the unfertilized flowers over a period of several weeks. Then the flowering pattern begins to change. The pistils begin to wither, similar to the way pistils of fertilized flowers do and they begin to dry while at the same time changing color. Next, the calyx (ovary) begins to swell. There is no seed developing inside the calyx; it is a sort of a false pregnancy. When the calyx has swelled, the cluster or cola is ripe and ready to be picked.

The pistil's color is a factor of genetics and temperature. Some plants, including many indicas, naturally develop a purplish color.

Female flowers show further development.

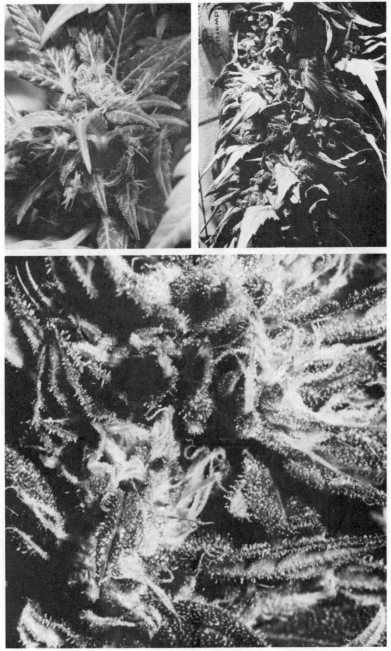

Mature female flowers.

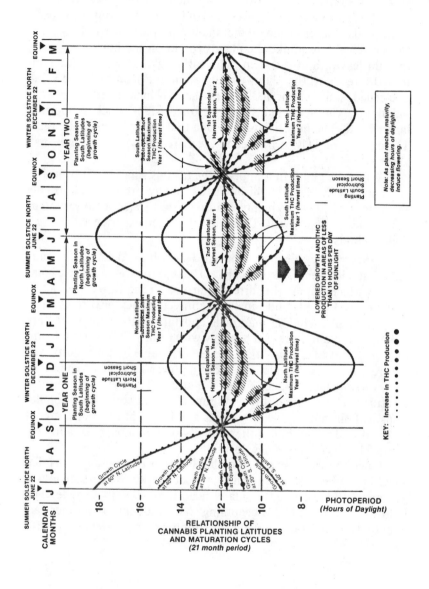

RELATIONSHIP OF
CANNABIS PLANTING LATITUDES
AND MATURATION CYCLES
(21 month period)

From MARIJUANA BOTANY © 1981 by R.C. Clarke, published by And/Or Press, Inc.

Many indicas and most sativas develop a red color. However, the color may change to purple or become more pronounced if the roots are subjected to a cool environment, below 55 degrees.

The growing flowers develop glands over their outer surfaces. Glands also develop along the small leaf parts surrounding the flower. These are unlike the glands found on the immature plant, the sun leaves, and the stem. The earlier glands were either connected directly to the plant, usually along the stem or had a small one-celled stalk connected to the head which filled with cannabinoids. The new glands have a longer stem which supports a larger head. The head is a membrane that fills with cannabinoids. The analogs of THC produced in the different types of glands may vary.

When the gland first appears the head is small but it begins to swell and looks like it might burst. Given any stress it will. Usually the head is filled as the plants go into the last stage of flowering, as the ovaries begin to swell. This is usually when experienced growers pick the buds.

Researchers, scientists, and gardeners have debated the purpose that THC serves to the plant. THC and the water-soluble compounds which impart the taste and aroma to the flowers act as an anti-bacterial agent, and repel some insects. They also repel most other animals including mammals and birds. (Remember, we are talking about a mature plant, heavy with resin.) This is not uncommon in plants. To assure that the seed is viable and not destroyed before it matures, the plant puts out a powerful array of chemicals to thwart predators. Once the seed matures, it is palatable to these creatures. This is one of the ways that the plant spreads its populations without human help. Animals and birds eat the seeds, an occasional seed passes out of the animal's system unharmed, allowing the species to colonize a new location.

Once the calyx swells, the glands begin to change color. The THC in the head was previously a clear liquid. When the calyx is getting a little overripe, the gland head tints an amber shade. This indicates that the THC is beginning to degrade into two other cannabinoids, CBL or CBN, which are not nearly as powerful as THC.

Chapter Twenty–Seven
Advanced Flowering

Created by Sam Selgnij
Copyright 1986 Ed Rosenthal and Sam Selgnij

In Chapter 25 (Flowering), marijuana's photoperiod response was described. Most varieties of cannabis flower in response to changes in the light cycle. This is a foolproof method for a plant to determine when to flower when it is adapted to a particular location. Every year the ratio of dark to light remains the same at a particular date. Scientists think that plants measure the number of hours of darkness by producing a hormone, tentatively named florigen. This hormone has not actually been discovered. The theory is that when the level of this hormone reaches a critical level, the plant goes into its reproductive mode.

Through simple experimentation, we know some interesting things about this plant response. It is a localized response by the plant. This was discovered by shading one branch of a plant but leaving the rest of it without a daily dark period. Only the branch that was shaded flowered. (This is a viable technique to use to sex plants).

Researchers think that the hormone is produced by the plant continuously. However, it is destroyed or metabolized by an enzyme or hormone which is produced only in the presence of light. Under natural conditions, the critical level builds up only with the onset of long nights in the autumn. When the dark cycle is interrupted by light, even for a few minutes or less, the florigen is destroyed by the plant and the plant starts the buildup to the critical level over again.

The response to different light cycles is a graduated one. Plants that initiate flowering at one light/darkness routine flower more heavily when the amount of darkness is increased. This response is more pronounced on plants originating from a higher latitude where the light cycle changes more.

Chrysanthemums are also long night-flowering plants, and their growth patterns have been studied extensively for use by the greenhouse industry. Researchers found that the largest flowers with the highest total weight were grown when the dark cycle routine was provided each night. When the plants were shaded 6 nights a week, there was a slight diminution of flower size and total weight. With each additional unshaded night, flower size and weight dropped.

Cannabis is one of the most widespread plants. It is naturalized everywhere from the equator to the arctic. (Private cannabis gardens have also been documented as being grown by scientists stationed at outposts in the Antarctic — it's not illegal there since no country has sovereignty). The plant has developed many variations on the photoperiod response to adjust to different climactic and latitudinal conditions.

Female plants from equatorial or sub-equatorial zones such as Colombia, southern Mexico, central Africa, and south India are absolute photo-determinate (APD). These plants are acclimated to latitudes in which there is little variation in the light cycle throughout the year. As long as the dark period falls below a minimum trigger period, the plant remains in the vegetative growth cycle. This can go on for years under continuous light conditions. When the dark period lengthens to a trigger point, the plant changes its growth pattern to sexual development. If the dark period falls below the trigger level when the plants are flowering, the plants easily revert back to vegetative growth.

APD plants are good candidates to flower and regenerate. Since they respond to the light cycle in a relatively simple way, irregular or interrupted cycles alter growth significantly. Buds are smaller, leafier, fluffier, looser, and may run. They look a bit like low-light flowers.

Flower size can be increased by allowing the plants to ripen fully, then placing them in a continuous light regimen for a few days. Flowering is triggered again and the plants produce new clusters of flowers.

Some cannabis varieties are "relative photoperiod determinate" (RPD). These plants have a trigger that they respond to under normal growing conditions, but when they receive an unusual light regimen, they respond to the change in the light conditions in unusual ways. For example, an early flowering indica normally triggers at 10 hours of darkness, but if it is grown under continuous light and then the darkness cycle is increased to 8 hours, the plant triggers. Once these plants are triggered, the light cycle has less affect upon them than upon the absolutes. The developing flowers are not as sensitive to occasional interruption of the darkness cycle.

RPD varieties include mid-and high-range latitude-adapted plants including Moroccans and southern Africans, early indicas, commercial hemp and hybrids developed for early harvest (September or earlier).

RPD varieties are harder to manipulate using the light cycle. Plants placed into flowering do not revert to vegetative growth as easily as APD varieties. The plants are harder to regenerate. Light stress promotes hermaphroditism in these varieties. They are harder to clone; they take longer and have a lower success rate.

Most males and some extreme northern varieties including the ruderalis strains fall into a third category which is not photosensitive at all. Both age and development seem to play a role in determining when these plants flower. For example, a Hungarian ruderalis developed flowers under continuous light after 8 weeks. Most varieties of males indicate under continuous light after 3-9 months. Thais and some equatorial sativa males are exceptions and will not flower until the dark period is increased. Under 18 hours of light, males indicate sooner than under continuous light.

Cold may hasten sexual expression but not flower development of some northern varieties.

Some varieties, especially indicas, respond to unnatural light cycles by showing of photo-period response disorder. Genetic females turn hermaphroditic when exposed to long dark periods during early growth.

Chart 27A

SUNRISE AND SUNSET			R = Sunrise
GREENWICH MEAN TIME			S = Sunset
			T = Total Hours of Light

LATITUDE ▶		0*	+10	+20	+30	+35	+40	+45	+50	+52	+54	+56	+58	+60
Jan 1st	= R	6:00	6:16	6:35	6:56	7:08	7:22	7:38	7:59	8:08	8:19	8:32	8:46	9:02
	= S	18:07	17:49	17:32	17:11	16:59	16:45	16:28	16:07	15:58	15:48	15:35	15:22	15:05
	= T	12:07	11:33	10:57	10:15	9:51	9:33	8:50	8:08	7:50	7:29	7:03	6:36	6:03
Jan 16	= R	6:06	6:21	6:38	6:59	7:08	7:20	7:34	7:52	8:01	8:10	8:20	8:33	8:47
	=S	18:13	17:57	17:42	17:23	17:12	16:59	16:45	16:27	16:19	16:09	15:59	15:47	15:33
	=T	12:07	11:36	11:06	10:24	10:04	9:39	9:11	8:35	8:18	7:59	7:39	7:14	6:46
Feb 1st	= R	6:10	6:23	6:36	6:51	7:00	7:09	7:21	7:35	7:41	7:48	7:56	8:05	8:15
	= S	18:17	18:04	17:51	17:37	17:28	17:19	17:08	16:53	16:46	16:39	16:32	16:24	16:14
	= T	12:07	11:41	11:15	10:46	10:28	10:00	9:47	9:18	9:03	8:51	8:36	8:19	7:59
Feb 16th	= R	6:11	6:20	6:29	6:40	6:46	6:52	7:00	7:10	7:14	7:19	7:25	7:30	7:37
	= S	18:18	18:08	17:59	17:49	17:43	17:36	17:28	17:19	17:15	17:09	17:04	16:59	16:52
	= T	12:07	11:48	11:30	11:09	10:57	10:44	10:28	10:09	10:01	9:50	9:39	9:29	9:15
Mar 1st	= R	6:09	6:14	6:19	6:25	6:28	6:32	6:36	6:41	6:44	6:46	6:48	6:51	6:55
	= S	18.16	18:10	18:06	18:00	17:57	17:53	17:49	17:44	17:42	17:39	17:36	17:33	17:30
	= T	12:07	11:56	11:47	11:35	11:29	11:21	11:13	11:03	10:58	10:43	9:48	9:42	9:35
Mar 16th	= R	6:06	6:08	6:07	6:08	6:09	6:10	6:10	6:12	6:12	6:12	6:12	6:13	6:14
	= S	18:12	18:11	18:10	18:09	18:09	18:08	18:08	18:07	18:07	18:07	18:06	18:06	18:05
	= T	12:06	12:03	12:03	12:03	12:01	12:00	11:58	11:58	11:55	11:55	11:55	11:54	11:49
Apr 1st	= R	6:01	5:57	5:53	5:49	5:47	5:44	5:40	5:37	5:35	5:33	5:31	5:28	5:25
	= S	18:07	18:11	18:14	18:19	18:22	18:24	18:28	18:32	18:34	18:36	18:38	18:41	18:43
	= T	12:06	12:14	12:21	12:30	12:35	12:40	12:48	12:55	12:59	13:03	13:07	13:13	13:18
Apr 16th	= R	5:57	5:49	5:41	5:32	5:26	5:21	5:13	5:05	5:01	4:57	4:52	4:46	4:40
	= S	18:03	18:10	18:19	18:29	18:34	18:39	18:47	18:56	18:59	19:04	19:09	19:14	19:21
	= T	12:06	12:21	12:38	12:57	13:08	13:18	13:34	13:51	13:58	14:07	14:17	14:28	14:41
May 1st	= R	5:54	5:43	5:31	5:17	5:09	5:00	4:49	4:36	4:30	4:23	4:14	4:08	3:56
	= S	18:00	18:11	18:24	18:37	18:45	18:55	19:05	19:19	19:26	19:34	19:41	19:41	20:01
	= T	12:06	12:28	12:53	13:20	13:36	13:55	14:16	14:43	14:56	15:11	15:27	15:33	16:05
May 16th	= R	5:53	5:39	5:24	5:06	4:56	4:45	4:31	4:14	4:06	3:57	3:47	3:36	3:22
	= S	18:00	18:14	18:29	18:47	18:57	19:08	19:22	19:39	19:48	19:57	20:07	20:18	20:32
	= T	12:07	12:35	13:05	13:41	14:01	14:23	14:51	15:25	15:42	16:00	16:20	16:42	17:10
Jun 1st	= R	5:54	5:38	5:20	5:00	4:48	4:34	4:17	3:56	3:46	3:36	3:23	3:09	2:51
	= S	18:01	18:17	18:36	18:56	19:08	19:22	19:39	19:59	20:09	20:20	20:33	20:48	21:06
	= T	12:07	12:39	13:16	13:56	14:20	14:48	15:22	16:03	16:23	16:44	17:10	17:39	18:15
Jun 16th	= R	5:56	5:39	5:20	4:58	4:45	4:30	4:13	3:50	3:39	3:27	3:13	2:57	2:36
	= S	18:04	18:21	18:40	19:02	19:15	19:31	19:49	20:11	20:12	20:34	20:48	21:04	21:26
	= T	12:07	12:42	13:20	14:04	14:30	15:01	15:36	16:21	16:33	17:07	17:35	18:07	18:50

* At the Equator, there is an additional 10 minutes of light before sunrise and after sunset. At higher latitudes during winter, there is an additional 10 minutes of light before sunrise and after sunset. During the summer, ambient light before sunrise and after sunset lasts considerably longer.

SUNRISE AND SUNSET   R = Sunrise
GREENWICH MEAN TIME   S = Sunset
                            T = Total Hours of Light

LATITUDE ►		0*	+10	+20	+30	+35	+40	+45	+50	+52	+54	+56	+58	+60
July 1st	= R	6:00	5:42	5:24	5:02	4:49	4:34	4:17	3:54	3:44	3:32	3:18	3:01	2:41
	= S	18:07	18:24	18:43	19:05	19:18	19:33	19:51	20:13	20:23	20:35	20:49	21:06	21:25
	= T	12:07	12:42	13:19	14:03	14:29	14:59	15:34	16:19	16:39	17:03	17:31	18:05	18:44
July 16th	= R	6:02	5:46	5:29	5:10	4:58	4:44	4:28	4:08	3:59	3:48	3:36	3:22	3:05
	= S	18:09	18:25	18:43	19:02	19:14	19:27	19:43	20:03	20:12	20:23	20:35	20:49	21:05
	= T	12:07	12:39	13:14	13:52	14:16	14:43	15:15	15:55	16:13	16:35	16:59	17:27	18:00
Aug 1st	= R	6:03	5:50	5:36	5:19	5:09	4:58	4:45	4:30	4:22	4:13	4:04	3:53	3:41
	= S	18:10	18:23	18:37	18:53	19:03	19:14	19:26	19:42	19:50	19:58	20:07	20:18	20:30
	= T	12:07	12:33	13:01	13:34	13:54	14:16	14:41	15:12	15:28	15:45	16:03	16:25	16:49
Aug 16th	= R	6:01	5:51	5:41	5:28	5:20	5:12	5:03	4:51	4:45	4:39	4:33	4:25	4:17
	= S	18:07	18:17	18:28	18:40	18:47	18:55	19:05	19:16	19:22	19:27	19:34	19:42	19:50
	= T	12:06	12:26	12:47	13:12	13:27	13:43	14:02	14:25	14:37	14:48	15:01	15:17	15:33
Sep 1st	= R	5:57	5:51	5:44	5:37	5:33	5:28	5:22	5:13	5:12	5:08	5:04	5:00	4:55
	= S	18:03	18:09	18:15	18:22	18:27	18:31	18:37	18:44	18:47	18:50	18:54	18:58	19:03
	= T	12:06	12:18	12:31	12:45	12:54	13:03	13:15	13:31	13:35	13:42	13:50	13:58	14:08
Sep 16th	= R	5:52	5:50	5:48	5:45	5:44	5:42	5:40	5:37	5:36	5:35	5:34	5:32	5:30
	= S	17:58	18:00	18:02	18:04	18:05	18:07	18:09	18:11	18:12	18:13	18:15	18:16	18:18
	= T	12:06	12:10	12:14	12:19	12:21	12:25	12:29	12:34	12:36	12:38	12:39	12:44	12:48
Oct 1st	= R	5:47	5:49	5:51	5:53	5:55	5:56	5:58	6:00	6:01	6:02	6:03	6:04	6:06
	= S	17:53	17:50	17:48	17:45	17:44	17:42	17:40	17:38	17:37	17:36	17:35	17:34	17:32
	= T	12:06	12:01	11:57	11:52	11:49	11:46	11:42	11:38	11:36	11:34	11:32	11:30	11:26
Oct 16th	= R	5:42	5:49	5:55	6:03	6:07	6:12	6:17	6:24	6:27	6:30	6:33	6:38	6:42
	= S	17:49	17:42	17:36	17:28	17:24	17:19	17:13	17:07	17:04	17:00	16:57	16:53	16:48
	= T	12:07	11:53	11:41	11:25	11:17	11:07	10:54	10:43	10:37	10:30	10:24	10:15	10:06
Nov 1st	= R	5:40	5:50	6:02	6:14	6:21	6:29	6:38	6:50	6:55	7:01	7:07	7:14	7:23
	= S	17:47	17:37	17:26	17:13	17:06	16:58	16:49	16:36	16:31	16:26	16:19	16:11	16:03
	= T	12:07	11:47	11:24	10:59	10:45	10:29	10:11	9:46	9:36	9:25	9:12	8:57	8:40
Nov 16th	= R	5:41	5:56	6:10	6:26	6:36	6:46	6:59	7:15	7:22	7:30	7:39	7:49	8:01
	= S	17:48	17:35	17:20	17:04	16:54	16:43	16:30	16:15	16:08	16:00	15:50	15:40	15:28
	= T	12:07	11:39	11:10	10:38	10:18	9:57	9:31	9:00	8:46	8:30	8:11	7:51	7:27
Dec 1st	= R	5:45	6:02	6:19	6:39	6:52	7:03	7:18	7:37	7:45	7:56	8:07	8:20	8:35
	= S	17:52	17:36	17:19	17:00	16:49	16:36	16:20	16:01	15:52	15:42	15:31	15:18	15:03
	= T	12:07	11:34	11:00	10:21	9:57	9:33	9:02	8:24	8:07	7:46	7:24	6:58	6:28
Dec 16th	= R	5:52	6:09	6:28	6:49	7:02	7:16	7:32	7:53	8:03	8:14	8:26	8:41	8:58
	= S	17:59	17:42	17:23	17:02	16:50	16:36	16:20	15:59	15:50	15:38	15:25	15:10	14:51
	= T	12:07	11:33	10:55	10:47	9:48	9:20	8:48	8:06	7:47	7:24	6:59	6:29	5:53

* At the Equator, there is an additional 10 minutes of light before sunrise and after sunset. At higher latitudes during winter, there is an additional 10 minutes of light before sunrise and after sunset. During the summer, ambient light before sunrise and after sunset lasts considerably longer.

Chart 27B
MATURATION PATTERNS UNDER NATURAL LIGHT
LENGTH OF FLOWERING

Inductions Flowering	3-4 Weeks Short	5-7 Weeks Medium	8-15 Weeks Long
Early July	1	2	3
Mid-August-September	4	5	6
Late October-November	7	8	9

Colombia & Equatorial African	8-9
South African	2
Southern Mexican	5-6
Early Indica	1-2
Late Indica	5
Southern Indian Sativa	8
Thai	9
Ruderalis	1
Nepalese	6
Chilean	1-2
Korean	1-2

Chart 27C
RUDERALIS

Hours of Daylight	Number of Days to Sex	Number of Weeks to Peak Fluorescence	Number of Weeks to Harvest
18			
17			
16			
15			
14			
13			
12			
11			
10			
9			
8			4

Chart 27D
COLOMBIAN
EQUATORIAL AFRICAN

Hours of Daylight	Number of Days to Sex	Number of Weeks to Peak Fluorescence	Number of Weeks to Harvest
18			
17			
16			
15			
14	18	11	13
13	17	10	12
12	16	9	11
11	15	8	10
10	14½	7	9
9	14	6	8
8	13	5	7

Chart 27E
THAI
SOUTHERN INDIAN SATIVA

Hours of Daylight	Number of Days to Sex	Number of Weeks to Peak Fluorescence	Number of Weeks to Harvest
18			
17			
16			
15			
14	23	13½	17
13	22	13	16
12	20	11½	14
11	18	10	13
10	16	9	12
9	14	7	10
8			

Chart 27F
SOUTH AFRICAN

Hours of Daylight	Number of Days to Sex	Number of Weeks to Peak Fluorescence	Number of Weeks to Harvest
18			
17			
16	15	8	9½
15	14	7	9
14	13	7	9
13	12	6	8½
12	10	6	8
11	9	5	7½
10	8	4	6
9	7	3½	5½
8	6	3	5

Chart 27G
LATE INDICA

Hours of Daylight	Number of Days to Sex	Number of Weeks to Peak Fluorescence	Number of Weeks to Harvest
18			
17			
16			
15	18	8	9½
14	17	7½	9
13	16	7	9
12	15	6½	8½
11	14	6	8
10	12	5	7½
9	10	5	7
8	9	4	6

Chart 27H
EARLY INDICA

Hours of Daylight	Number of Days to Sex	Number of Weeks to Peak Fluorescence	Number of Weeks to Harvest
18			
17			
16	14	6	8
15	13	6	8
14	12	5½	7
13	11	5	7
12	10	4½	6½
11	9	4	6
10	8	3½	5
9	7	3	5
8	6	2½	4½

Chart 27I
NEPALESE

Hours of Daylight	Number of Days to Sex	Number of Weeks to Peak Fluorescence	Number of Weeks to Harvest
18			
17			
16			
15	16	8	10
14	15	7	9½
13	14	7	9
12	13	6	8½
11	12	6	8
10	10	5	7½
9	9	5	7
8	8	4	6

Chart 27J
SOUTHERN MEXICAN

Hours of Daylight	Number of Days to Sex	Number of Weeks to Peak Fluorescence	Number of Weeks to Harvest
18			
17			
16			
15	14	7	9
14	13	7	9
13	13	6	8
12	12	6	8
11	11	5	7½
10	10	5	7
9	9	4	6½
8	9	4	6

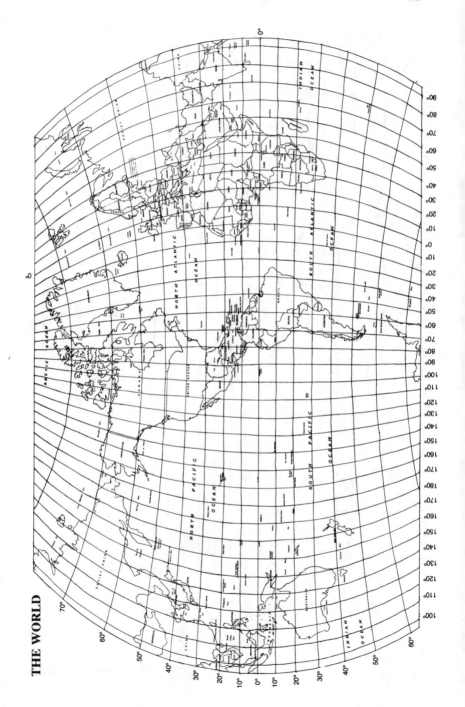

THE WORLD

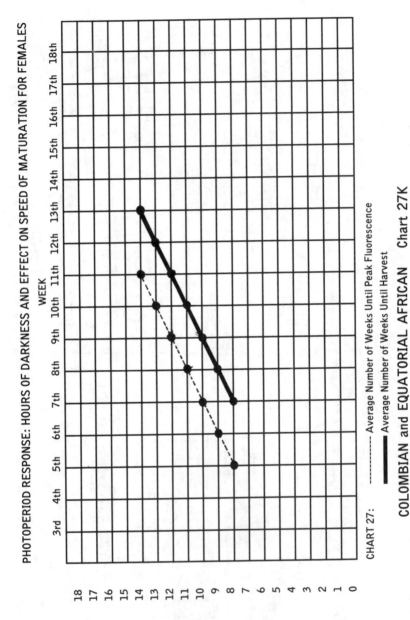

PHOTOPERIOD RESPONSE: HOURS OF DARKNESS AND EFFECT ON SPEED OF MATURATION FOR FEMALES

HOURS OF DAYLIGHT

WEEK

CHART 27:   ----------- Average Number of Weeks Until Peak Fluorescence

━━━━━ Average Number of Weeks Until Harvest

COLOMBIAN and EQUATORIAL AFRICAN   Chart 27K

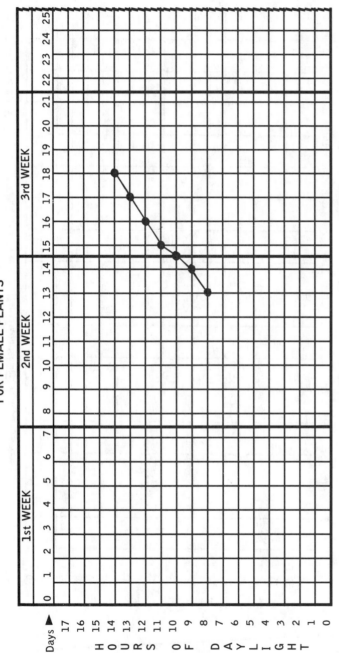

AVERAGE NUMBER OF DAYS TO INDUCE SEX AND START FLOWERING FOR FEMALE PLANTS

COLOMBIAN and EQUATORIAL AFRICAN — Chart 27L

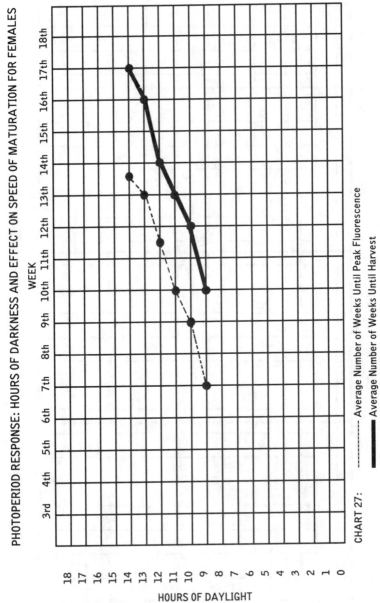

PHOTOPERIOD RESPONSE: HOURS OF DARKNESS AND EFFECT ON SPEED OF MATURATION FOR FEMALES

WEEK

HOURS OF DAYLIGHT

CHART 27:   ------- Average Number of Weeks Until Peak Fluorescence
             ▬▬▬ Average Number of Weeks Until Harvest

THAI and SOUTHERN INDIAN SATIVA Chart 27M

AVERAGE NUMBER OF DAYS TO INDUCE SEX AND START FLOWERING
FOR FEMALE PLANTS

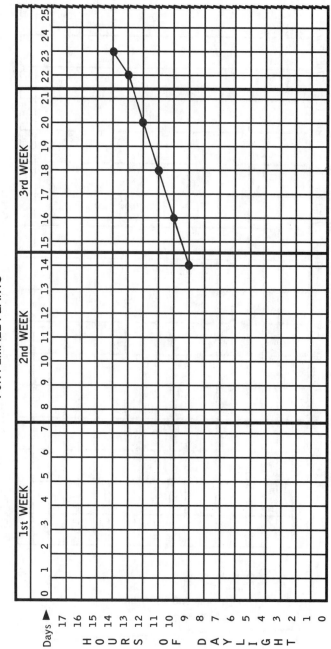

THAI and SOUTHERN INDIAN SATIVA - Chart 27N

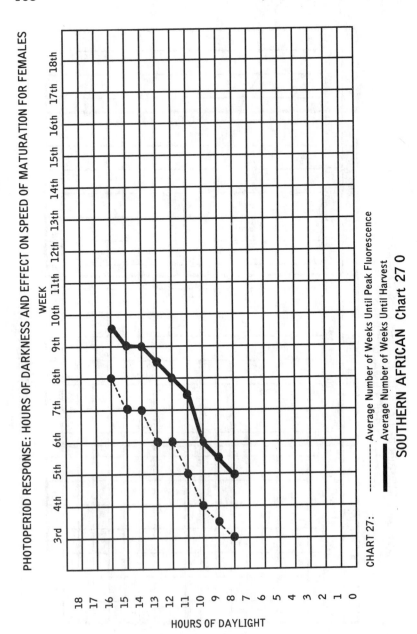

PHOTOPERIOD RESPONSE: HOURS OF DARKNESS AND EFFECT ON SPEED OF MATURATION FOR FEMALES

WEEK

HOURS OF DAYLIGHT

CHART 27:

--------- Average Number of Weeks Until Peak Fluorescence

Average Number of Weeks Until Harvest

SOUTHERN AFRICAN   Chart 27 0

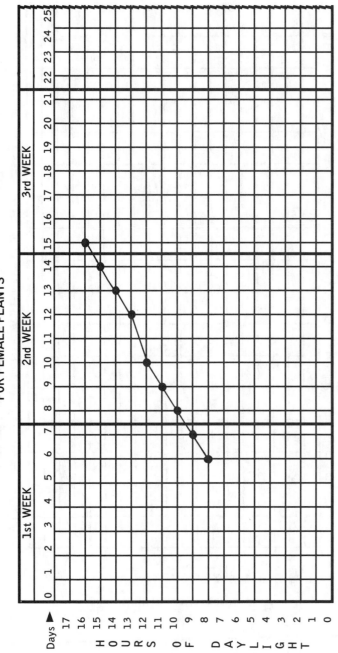

AVERAGE NUMBER OF DAYS TO INDUCE SEX AND START FLOWERING FOR FEMALE PLANTS

SOUTHERN AFRICAN — Chart 27P

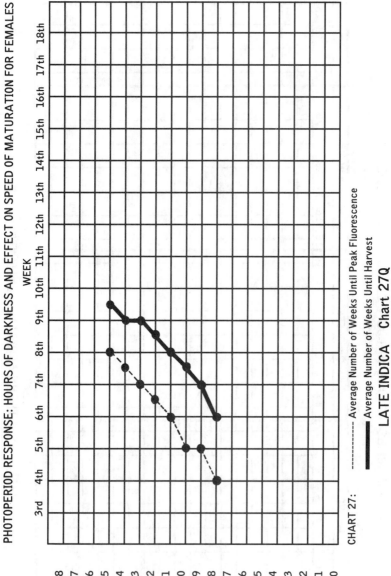

PHOTOPERIOD RESPONSE: HOURS OF DARKNESS AND EFFECT ON SPEED OF MATURATION FOR FEMALES

CHART 27:

------- Average Number of Weeks Until Peak Fluorescence

——— Average Number of Weeks Until Harvest

LATE INDICA   Chart 27Q

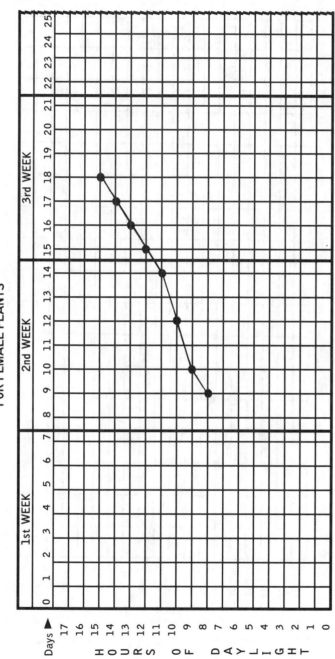

AVERAGE NUMBER OF DAYS TO INDUCE SEX AND START FLOWERING FOR FEMALE PLANTS

LATE INDICA — Chart 27R

PHOTOPERIOD RESPONSE: HOURS OF DARKNESS AND EFFECT ON SPEED OF MATURATION FOR FEMALES

CHART 27:   ----------- Average Number of Weeks Until Peak Fluorescence
            —————— Average Number of Weeks Until Harvest

EARLY INDICA   Chart 27 S

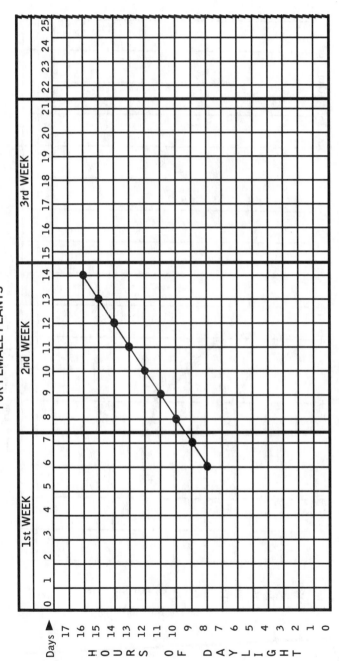

AVERAGE NUMBER OF DAYS TO INDUCE SEX AND START FLOWERING FOR FEMALE PLANTS

EARLY INDICA — Chart 27 T

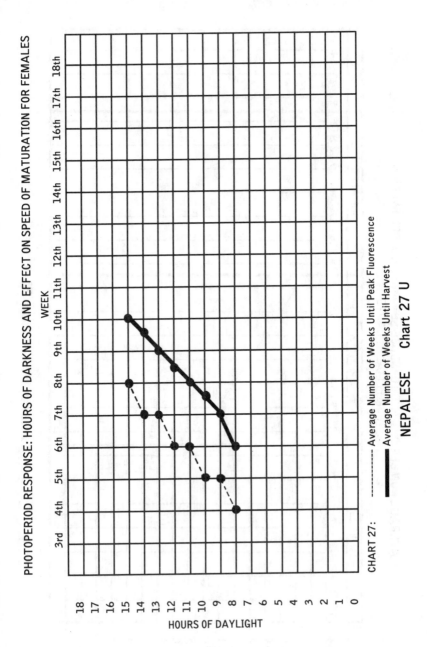

PHOTOPERIOD RESPONSE: HOURS OF DARKNESS AND EFFECT ON SPEED OF MATURATION FOR FEMALES

CHART 27:   --------- Average Number of Weeks Until Peak Fluorescence
             _____ Average Number of Weeks Until Harvest

NEPALESE   Chart 27 U

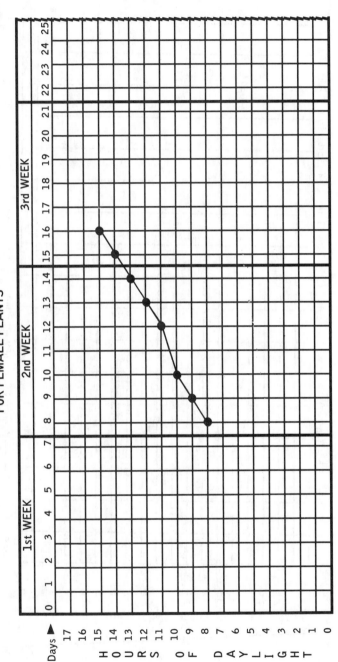

AVERAGE NUMBER OF DAYS TO INDUCE SEX AND START FLOWERING
FOR FEMALE PLANTS

NEPALESE — Chart 27 V

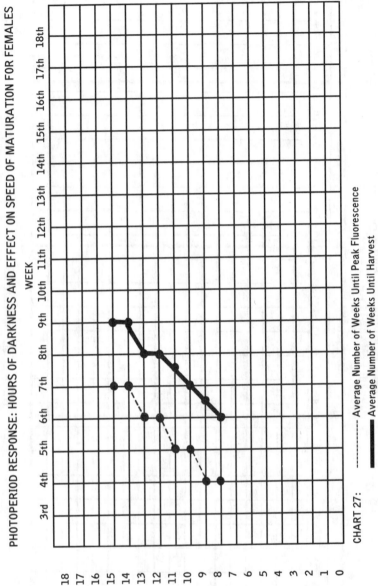

PHOTOPERIOD RESPONSE: HOURS OF DARKNESS AND EFFECT ON SPEED OF MATURATION FOR FEMALES

WEEK

HOURS OF DAYLIGHT

CHART 27:   ---------- Average Number of Weeks Until Peak Fluorescence

            ━━━━━ Average Number of Weeks Until Harvest

SOUTHERN MEXICAN   Chart 27 W

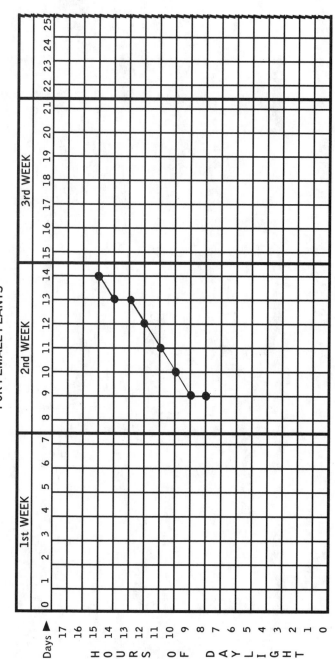

AVERAGE NUMBER OF DAYS TO INDUCE SEX AND START FLOWERING FOR FEMALE PLANTS

SOUTHERN MEXICAN — Chart 27 X

Chapter Twenty–Eight

Breeding

Humans have been breeding marijuana informally for thousands of years. The first farmers chose seeds from the best plants. Over many generations the plant was differentiated into varieties which had different uses and thrived under various environmental conditions.

Scientific breeding did not begin until Gregor Mendel's experiments on inherited characteristics were discovered. Mendel crossed peas with differing characteristics and found that the offspring plants inherited traits from their parents in a logical, predictable, statistical way.

Today we know that each cell contains a set of chemical blueprints regarding every aspect of its existence. These chemical codes are called chromosomes and they consist of long double strands of sugar which have "bases" consisting of one of four amino acids. Sets of three of these amino acid bases form genes which are "read" by structures in the cell and direct it in its life processes.

Chromosomes are found in pairs in most cells. Half of each pair of chromosomes is contributed by the male through pollen and half by the female. Marijuana has 10 pairs or 20 chromosomes. Each chromosome's genes are lined up in a specific order. The other member of the pair has a corresponding gene in the same location. Sometimes, a single gene is responsible for a characteristic. In other cases, several genes are responsible, often in a complex series of reactions.

There has been very little formal genetic work on marijuana. Almost all of the research is the result of observation by cultivators. However, the cell and its chromosomes are easily observed using a high-powered microscope. Even an inexpensive instrument allows one to see the chromosomes during mitosis (cell division). The chromosomes line up in pairs and then reproduce themselves as the cell splits into two. When reproductive cells are produced, the pairs of chromosomes split and only one chromosome of each pair goes into each reproductive cell. (Photographs can be taken with the aid of a 35 mm SLR camera and an inexpensive adapter tube.)

About 2% of the time, the genes "jump" from one member of the pair of chromosomes to the other. This is a significant fact in breeding because it gives individual chromosomes a means of changing information regarding the characteristics for which they are coded.

Breeding would be a relatively simple task if only one trait or characteristic were involved. However there are many factors to consider when choosing plants for breeding. These include: potency, taste, aroma, color, maturation time, yield, height, branching habits, adaption to low-light conditions, resistance to pests or diseases, leaf drop at maturity, and sterility.

When a plant "breeds true" it means that most of the corresponding genes on each of the pairs of chromosomes of the 10 pairs have the same information. However, plants of different varieties which are crossed are hybrids, and many of the corresponding genes on the two sets of chromosomes have information which is in conflict. For instance, the first generation cross (an F_1 hybrid) may contain genes from one parent programmed for tall plants and genes from the other parent programmed for short stature. In this case the plants all have approximately the same height, intermediate between the two parents. When two F_1 hybrids are crossed, however, the plants are either tall, intermediate or short. The reason is that some of the plants have genes for tallness, some for shortness and others for both.

Many of the important characteristics of marijuana seem to be coded for "partial dominance" as was just described. Aroma, taste, and potency seem to fall into this category. When more than one gene is involved, there can be enormous numbers of possible combinations.

Some characteristics are coded on genes which are either dominant or recessive. According to Robert Connell Clarke, author of *Marijuana Botany*, tall height, unwebbed leaves, green rather than purple coloring on calyxes (seed bracts), and large-size seeds are all dominant genes. A cross between two plants with conflicting genes would result in the F_1 generation all showing the dominant trait. A cross between two F_1 plants results in a majority of the plants indicating the dominant trait and only a few, those without the dominant gene on either chromosome, indicating the information found on the recessive gene.

It is difficult for the hobbyist or grower to institute a scientific breeding program because thousands of plants must be grown to find one specimen which meets ideal breeding requirements. Growers have a limited amount of space to devote to the plants and thus have trouble sorting out the crosses. Cultivators can select the best plants in the garden for breeding. Sometimes a plant has one outstanding characteristic but is unexceptional in other respects. This characteristic can be introduced into the breeding pool and then the undesirable traits can be "sorted out".

Marijuana is especially difficult to breed scientifically because half the plants, those bearing pollen, carry genetic information for hidden factors. An observer has few means of judging the genetic potential of male plants regarding yield, bud structure, and even potency. There is some correlation between the male's potency and that of its daughters. One way to solve this problem is to induce male flowers on female plants. Then the characteristics of both parents are known and all the resulting plants have only female chromosomes.

As in humans, gender in cannabis is determined by the "X" and "Y" chromosomes. The female has two X chromosomes and the male has one X and one Y. When the male plant produces pollen, half of the reproductive cells receive X and half Y. However, when male flowers are artificially induced in female plants, the pollen contains only X chromosomes, the only sex chromosomes the female plant has. All the resulting seeds contain two X chromosomes, one from each parent.

To induce male flowers in female plants, the plants are sprayed with gibberellic acid or watered with an aspirin/water solution.

Gibberellic acid is a plant hormone originally isolated from mold-infested rice. Symptoms of the infection include extraordinary vertical growth. Gibberellic acid affects plants in a variety of ways. In marijuana, it causes extension of all stems on which it is sprayed, and if used before flowers develop, it occasionally induces "sex reversal" in females: male flowers develop on sprayed areas. The plant's genetic structure remains the same; however, the sex characteristics are altered. In a general way this is similar to a sex change operation; the genetic information contains information for one sex, but the hormones which are introduced by pill or injection artificially induce physiological changes in the body, including development of the other sex's sexual characteristics.

Several correspondents have described the results of adding aspirin to their water. One grower used two aspirin in a gallon of water when the plants were in their third week of flowering. He said that the plants grew thousands of pollen sacs which contained fertile pollen.

The most methodical way to breed marijuana using these substances is to allow the plants to flower after taking several clones from each plant. Once the plants are harvested, cured and tested, the cuttings of all except those plants selected as the best for breeding are eliminated. When the plants are large enough to produce adequate amounts of seed for the breeder's purpose, some of the plants are kept as females, and male flowers are induced in others. Then the plants are bred.

The first step involves gathering the pollen. Since cannabis is usually wind-pollinated, it produces an abundance of pollen which floats easily in the air. The male plants are placed in a separate draft-free location and the pollen drops onto unprinted paper placed underneath the plant. However, if there are several plants in the same room, the different plants' pollen may become contaminated with each other. If the plants are bent or turned on their sides so that the pollen has to drop through less air, more pollen collects. Plants placed in a cardboard box are even less susceptible to draft.

Some growers collect pollen by cutting the flower spikes off the plants just as the flowers are to open. These spikes are placed in a paper bag so no pollen is lost. Pollen can also be collected by placing a white paper bag around flower spikes. White paper is used so that light rays are reflected rather than absorbed by the bag and turned into heat, which may damage the plant. Non-coated parchment paper breathes and eliminates humidity problems.

Once the pollen is collected, the female flowers are fertilized. (If pollen is scarce, it is diluted 10–100 parts by weight with flour). Pollination can be accomplished simply by placing a bag filled with pollen around a bud and then shaking it. The pollen settles for a day or two and then is removed. Another method is to "paint" the pollen onto the female flowers using a small watercolor brush. One grower insists that it is easiest to pollinate using your fingers.

The best time to pollinate marijuana is when the flowers are well developed but still fresh, and have gone through several stages of growth and filling out.

Breeding is a very detailed subject and this is just a cursory discussion of it. For more information, I recommend the book, *Marijuana Botany* by R.C. Clarke.

Chapter Twenty–Nine
Harvesting

Female marijuana goes through several stages of flowering. First a few flowers appear. Then new flowers develop around the first ones. Flowers also form at each leaf node along the branches and main stem. The buds start to fill out so that the cluster becomes thick with pistils (the little antennae) reaching out for pollen. The pistils are white, or sometimes shaded pink or lavender. They look fresh and moist.

Some of the pistils begin to wither and turn red, purple, or even a light brown. Just as the cluster looks like it's finished, a new wave of flower growth appears, usually concentrated in a relatively bare spot. Successive waves of flowers may appear for weeks.

The flowers close, and the calyxes start to swell. This is a false seed pod; the flowers have not been fertilized and no seed can develop. These pods are totally covered with resin glands. At maturity the glands should sparkle like individual jewels in bright light. The individual glands should appear clear under magnification. When the glands turn amber, the buds should be harvested.

No bud should be picked before its time. Plants and varieties differ as to maturation pattern. Some plants mature all at once, so that the whole plant can be picked. Other varieties mature from the top down. One respected researcher claimed "Most plants I've had mature bottom to top. The main bud was the last to finish." Under lights, however, the top buds mature first most of the time. Next, the buds nearest the top and so on. The buds on the outside of the branch are likely to mature faster than inner buds. It may take a month before the plant is totally picked. Picking the plant a little at a time allows previously shaded portions of the plant to receive light and grow.

A HARVEST PROBLEM

Some equatorial varieties need so much light to mature proper-
ly that it is virtually impossible to supply the intensity using artificial light as the only source. These plants grow flowers but the
growth is loose and the flowers take months to ripen. Sometimes
the flowers "run". They grow very sparsely along the stem instead
of forming tight clusters. Increasing the amount of light helps. One
grower said that lowering the temperature in the grow room encourages the plants to develop more compact growth.

Although these equatorial buds may not look great, and have
less commercial value, they may still be extremely potent and be
genetically coded for the soaring sativa high.

Usually, indoor flowers are not as compact as outdoor grown
flowers. They are every bit as potent though, perhaps more potent.
Outdoors, plants are subject to a harsh environment. Wind, rain,
animals passing through, plant and animal droppings all take their
toll on THC glands. They are punctured, rubbed off or even washed away. Indoors, plants are living in a friendlier environment and
almost all of the glands produced remain on the plant. The more
glands present, the stronger the grass.

MOLD

Dense buds are sometimes attacked by molds. These fast-growing, non-green plants grow from spores which float in the air. They start to grow when they come in contact with a conducive environment: high humidity, low light and temperatures in the 60's. These conditions are most likely to occur outdoors or in a greenhouse during harvest season, when the temperatures are lower than during the summer and when there is less light and higher humidity from the dense foliage. Any moisture or wetness is easily trapped in the buds and the molds grow quickly, turning a beautiful bud into mush or slime overnight.

Indoors, molds also occur during harvest season, usually due to low light conditions and too high a humidity.

There are several things that can be done to prevent molds, and to limit the damage that they do. Molds are much less likely to grow when the temperature is above their ideal conditions. By keeping the space in the high 70's, their growth may be prevented. Since the spores float in the air, they can be precipitated using a negative ion generator. This means that there are fewer agents to create infections. Lowering the humidity by using a dehumidifier or air vent stops the growth.

Once mold occurs in the space, the farmer should take action immediately. The mold's growth can be stopped by raising temperature and lowering humidity. Increasing light intensity helps. All buds which show signs of mold damage should be harvested. Some growers cut the infected material out of buds instead of removing the entire piece. The site of the infection can be sprayed with a 5% bleach solution to kill the remaining mold. This need not be rinsed.

Some growers use commercial fungicides available for various molds, but many of these are not recommended for food plants and others have long residual life.

Chapter Thirty
Curing and Manicuring

When a bud is picked, many of its metabolic processes continue for a while. The cells begin to convert carbohydrates back to sugars and break down some of the pigments. Chlorophyll is one of the pigments affected. Some of it is metabolized and the bud appears a lighter green than when it was first picked. Some of the other pigments will show through then, giving the bud a red, purple or cream color.

To continue to cure, the leaves need to be dried slowly so that moisture remains in the cells. They stay alive and continue life processes. On the other hand, if the curing process takes too long, mold may form on the buds.

Small amounts of marijuana dissipate their water quickly in an open room because the relative humidity of the air in houses is usually dry. A paper bag can be used to conserve water. The bag should be opened and aired twice a day. In areas with high humidity or when it is rainy, there is enough moisture in the air to let the buds dry in the open air.

Bringing in the legal harvest in India.

Larger amounts are cured in areas with more air circulation —
an attic or basement or a dark room will do. A fan may be needed
to increase circulation. Since all of the vegetation is contributing
moisture to the air, ventilation is needed to remove it. Rooms that
are too moist are conducive to mold. If mold appears, increase the
heat in the room to 80 degrees, so that the air can absorb more
water.

Whole plants can be hung upside down but it is much easier to
hang branches cut in 1–2 foot lengths. These can be hung along
lines, laid on trays or placed on shelves. It is easy to hang buds using
clothespins or twist-ties.

Some growers don't mind a little more chlorophyll taste and
would rather dry the buds quickly. If the space has low humidity
and is warm, the plants will dry fast. One grower placed buds in a
microwave oven for 30 seconds or more on high power so that some
of the moisture was removed, then let them dry normally. He said it
reduced drying time by 50%. Microwaves kill seeds, so that buds
containing desired seed should not be microwaved.

Food dehydrators can come in handy, too. They never get very
hot so little THC is destroyed, yet their warmth promotes quick
drying. Some growers let the plants dry naturally for a few days and
then finish them off in the food dryer.

If plants begin to mold, they should be dried immediately before the infection can spread. Mold is contained by keeping infected plants separated from others. This should always be done because of latent spores.

Drying in an oven is not recommended. Getting the timing wrong or forgetting the buds for a few minutes can spell disaster. A vegetable dehydrator serves the purpose much better because it has relatively low maximum temperatures and will not burn the buds.

While the plants are drying, the large leaves can be removed using scissors, a knife, fingernails, or a clipper. It is harder and takes longer to manicure when the plants are wet.

The best time to manicure is when the plants are near dry. When the plants are wet they are difficult to clip. When they are dry many of the glands fall off as the bud is handled. When the plants still have some moisture, the glands are more likely to stay attached to the plant. Manicuring is easier right after picking because the leaves are still turgid. Growers sometimes manicure while the plants are still standing. The plants are in a convenient position and there seems to be less chance of damage to the bud.

(A) First the large leaves are removed,

(B) then the smaller leaves are tackled.

Buds which are too close can be pressed together when they are still wet. They will dry in the position they hold. Rolling them gently in between one's hands shapes them.

Plenty of light must be used manicuring the buds so that the grower can see clearly exactly what he is doing. A good overhead light as well as a table or floor lamp will do as long as it is bright. A directional light such as an office or typewiter lamp is ideal.

To manicure, the large sun leaves outside of the bud area are removed. The smaller multi-fingered leaves are removed next. The bud should now appear almost naked, except for some single fingered leaves sticking out from between the flowers. Rather than removing these leaves entirely, they are clipped down to the cir-cumference of the flowers, so that the ends of the leaf do not stick out.

Once the bud has dried, it should be packed in an airtight, lightight container. Buds which are packed moist are likely to mold. One grower left some moisture on the buds, packed them in food

Close-up of buds.

sealers, and then microwaved them to kill the mold. A bud should be left undisturbed until it is to be smoked. Every time it is moved, unpacked, or handled, some of the resin glands fall off. The glands can be seen cascading through the air whenever a bud is handled roughly.

Sun leaves are unsuitable for smoking except through a water-pipe. The leaves can be prepared for smoking by soaking them in water for several hours and then rinsing the leaves. The water dissolves many of the pigments and resins including much of the chlorophyll, but the THC remains on the leaves. The water is dumped and then the leaves are dried. They smoke much smoother than they did originally. They can also be used in cooking, in brewing or the THC they hold can be removed and concentrated.

The smaller leaves which were trimmed from the buds, including single finger leaves and trimming, are quite potent but they do not smoke that smoothly. Trim can also be smoked in a water-pipe or soaked in water.

Kitten inspecting buds, trim, leaf and stem from single plant.

The buds are usually saved for smoking. The quality of the bud improves for several weeks after it has dried. The THC acid loses its water molecule and becomes psychoactive. Once the bud is fairly dry, the evaporation can be speeded up by keeping the bud in a warm place for a few hours or by using a microwave oven.

This flowering plant was regenerated into vegetative stage.

Chapter Thirty–One
Regeneration

After the marijuana plant has ripened and the flowers have reached full maturity, it still responds to changes in its environment. Plants can be regenerated and can yield a second, third and possibly even more harvests.

In its natural environment, marijuana flowers in the fall, and then dies as the environment becomes inhospitable and the number of daylight hours decrease. However, if the daylength increases, the plants soon begin to revert from flowering to vegetative growth. At first, the plant produces single-fingered leaves, then 3 and 5 fingered leaves. Within a few weeks the plants grow at the rapid vegetative rate.

There are several advantages to regenerating marijuana plants rather than starting from seed. The plant has been harvested and its qualities and potency are known. The plant has already built its infrastructure. Its root system and main stem are already grown so that it takes less energy and time for the plant to produce new vegetative growth. A regenerated plant produces the same amount of vegetative growth in 45 days that takes a plant started from seed 75 days.

To regenerate a plant, some leaves and bud material are left on the stem as the plant is harvested. The stem may be left at nearly its full length, or cut back to only a few inches from the ground. The more stem with leaf material left on the plant, the faster it regenerates, as new growth develops at the sites of the remaining leaf material.

The plant started flowering in response to a change in the light cycle. To stop the flowering process, the light cycle is turned back to a long day period. The plant reacts as if it had lived through the winter and renews growth as if it were spring. Within 7–10 days new non-flowering growth is apparent.

Marijuana seems to react fastest to the change in light cycle when the light is kept on continually during the changeover period. After it has indicated new growth, the light cycle may be adjusted to the normal garden lighting cycle.

Chapter Thirty–Two
Cloning

Clones are a fancy name for cuttings. Almost everyone has taken a piece of a plant and placed it in water until it grew roots. As it developed, the leaves, flowers, fruit and other characteristics of the plant were exactly the same as the donor plant from which it was taken. That cutting was an exact genetic reproduction of a donor plant.

Many growers prefer to start their garden from clones. There are several reasons for this.

Growers must start only a few more plants than needed because all the clones, being the same genetic make-up, are the same sex as the donor, presumably, female.

Clone gardens are usually derived from donors which were exceptional plants. The new plants are every bit as exceptional as the donor.

The plants have the same growth and flowering patterns, maturation time, nutrient requirements, taste and high. The garden has a uniformity that allows the grower to use the space most efficiently.

Unique plants with rare genetic characteristics can be saved genetically intact. For example, a grower had an infertile female. Even though the plant was in the midst of a mixed field, it produced no seed. At the end of the season the plant was harvested and that rare quality died with the plant. Had the grower made cuttings, that plant's traits would have been preserved.

Clone gardens have disadvantages, too. If a disease attacks a garden, all of the plants have the same susceptibility because they all have the same qualities of resistance. The home gardener may get tired of smoking the same stuff all of the time. In terms of genetics, the garden is stagnant; there is no sexual reproduction taking place.

Cuttings root easiest when they are made while the plant is still in its vegetative growth stage. However, they can be taken even as the plant is being harvested. Some growers think that cuttings from the bottom of the plant, which gets less light, are better clone material, but cuttings from all parts of the plant can root.

Cuttings are likely to have a high dropoff rate if they are not given a moist, warm environment. They often succumb to stem rot or dehydration. Stem rot is usually caused by a lack of oxygen. Dehydration results from improper irrigation techniques, letting the medium dry, or from overtaxing the new plants. Cuttings do not have the root system required to transpire large amounts of water needed under bright light conditions. Instead, they are placed in a moderately lit area where their resources are not stressed to the limit.

Growers who are making only 1 or 2 cuttings usually take the new growth at the ends of the branches. These starts are 4–6 inches long. All of the large leaves are removed and vegetative growth is removed except for an inch of leaves and shoots at the end-tip. If large numbers of cuttings are being taken, a system using less donor-plant material is preferred. Starts can be made from many of the internodes along the branch which have vegetative growth. These starts are at least an inch long and each one has some leaf material.

If the cuttings are not started immediately, air may get trapped at the cut end, preventing the cutting from obtaining water. To prevent this, ⅛ inch is sliced off the end of the stem immediately before planting or setting to root.

All cuts should be made with a sterile knife, scissors, or razor blade. Utensils can be sterilized using bleach, fire, or alcohol. Some horticulturists claim that scissors squeeze and injure remaining tissue, but this does not seem to affect survival rates.

Stem is trimmed, dusted with fungicide, hormone mix, and then placed in medium.
Photos by G. Demarest

It usually takes between 10 and 20 days for cuttings to root. They root fastest and with least dropoff when the medium is kept at about 65 degrees.

Small cuttings can be rooted in water by floating them. The "Klone Kit", which is no longer available, used small styrofoam chips, which are sold as packing material, to hold the cuttings. Holes were placed in the chips with a pencil or other sharp instrument, and then the stem slipped through. The unit easily floats in the water. The kit also included rooting solution, 100 milliliter plastic cups (3 ounce), and coarse vermiculite. The cups were half filled with vermiculite and then the water-rooting solution was poured to the top of the cups. As the water level lowered, the cuttings rooted in the vermiculite.

Styrofoam chips can be floated in the water without solid medium. When the cuttings begin to root, they are moved to vermiculite. One grower adapted this technique using one-holed cork stoppers instead of styrofoam chips. He used 1 x 2 inch, 72-unit seed trays and placed one cork in each unit.

The water is changed daily, or a small air pump can be used to supply air to the water, so that the submerged plant parts have access to oxygenated water. A water-soluble rooting agent containing B_1 and the rooting hormone indolebutyric acid promote root growth. A very dilute nutrient solution which is relatively high in P is added to the water once roots appear. When the cutting develops roots, it can be planted in a moist medium such as vermiculite and watered with a dilute nutrient solution for 10–15 days.

One popular commercial cloning kit consists of a tray which holds peat pellets in a miniature greenhouse. The cuttings are placed one to a peat pellet. Fairly small-to-large-size cuttings can be placed in these pellets.

Cuttings can be rooted in the same way as any other woody cutting. First, the branch is cut into two, including some foliage on the upper segment of the branch. Smaller cuttings can be made, but they are harder to manipulate. Then a diagonal cut is made at the bottom end of the shoot. The cutting is put into a unit of 1 x 2″, 72-cup seed trays, 2″ pot or 6 ounce styrofoam cup filled with fine vermiculite wetted to saturation with water containing a rooting solution such as Klone Concentrate™.

To place the cutting in the medium without scraping off the fungicide, a thin pencil or other rod is pushed into the medium, creating a hole. The cutting is gently placed in the hole and the medium gently pressed down tightly around the stem so that there is moist contact.

Cuttings do best and have a much higher survival rate when they are rooted in a humid atmosphere. The tray or containers are covered with a clear plastic cover which keeps moisture high and allows the light in. The cuttings are kept warm and within a few weeks they develop into rootlings. One grower used a pyrex dish and cover to root her cuttings which were placed in 1½ inch square containers.

A commercial rooting kit no longer available. The home hobbyist can duplicate the kit using plastic cups, vermiculite and styrofoam chips. Rooting hormone was also included.

Chapter Thirty–Three
Marijuana Question?
Ask Ed

My objective in writing MGH was to provide the gardener a comprehensive guide to cultivation. However, no book can cover all the circumstances that can happen in a garden. This is why the "Ask Ed" colum is so educational for both the readers and myself. Circumstances and situations which we wouldn't imagine are described, ideas circulated and results reported. On the other hand, I receive some questions repeatedly. This is important, too, because it guides the column's direction.

While MGH is very comprehensive, it is a general book, and your garden is specific. After rereading the book I thought that it would be more complete if questions of importance to readers not specifically discussed, were answered in a question and answer section. This will help other gardeners with their gardens. I hope you find the section helpful and helps you avoid mistakes and solve problems, or even just pique or satisfy your curiosity.

If you have question, tips, information or researh on marijuana, its cultivation and the culture surrounding it to ASK ED, POB 429477, SF, CA 94142. E-Mail: ASKED@ WELL. COM

TOP 10 STUPID GROWER TRICKS 12/96

I thought I'd share this top 10 list with you.

10. Drive to the grow supply store in the car registered at the garden's home address.
9. Purchase all growing supplies by phone and have them sent to the garden address.
8. Tell two friends. They will be sure to tell two friends who will be sure to...
7. Invite everyone to the garden for "an after hours party."
6. Mess with your best friend's lover.
5. Mess with anyone if your lover finds out.

4. Plant a plot 2 blocks from the municipal airport.
3. Make yourself known to the local cops by speeding, or other lame traffic violations, bar-room scenes or other nasty habits.
2. Smoke fatties when there's a major drought and you are the only one with reefer.
1. Talk about what a great grower you are and the great success of your last garden.

Pele, Aloha, OR

———

Thanks for the list, Pele.

Sound & Smell Problems

LOUD BALLAST 5/92

Dear Ed,

I have a 1000 watt MH lamp. The ballast creates a loud buzzing hum. Are all ballasts noisy or is something wrong? Any suggestions on how to reduce or eliminate the noise?

Buzz W., St. Louis, MO

———

Some brands are noisier than others. However, individual ballasts from the same brand also vary in noise level. Perhaps the box is noisy because vibration is the result of a loose connection in the ballast box. Have an electrical technician check it and tighten everything up. This may eliminate some noise. To minimize the sound, place the ballast on a surface which does not vibrate. Foam pads under the ballast help absorb some of the vibrations and lower noise intensity.

A sound box made from egg cartons or acoustical tile will also help dampen the sound.

ION GENERATORS OR AIR CLEANERS

Dear Ed,

Is the activated carbon-filter (acf) in my new air cleaner-negative ion generator effective, or would I be just as well off with a simple negative ion generator? Will the acf absorb CO_2, slowing ripening? Does it absorb odor?

My 5' x 5' x 7' chamber is very clean. Does the dust that collects on the acf qualify as hash?

Do negative ion generators in proximity to the plants diminish their potency?

New Frontiersman, Portland, OR

———

As you noticed, the acf has collected dust. That means that it is effective at screening dust from the air. Obviously, the combination of negative ion generator and air cleaner is more effective than air cleaner or ionizer alone. The activated charcoal absorbs no CO_2 and will not affect plant growth adversely.

Odor is caused by solid particles floating in the air. They are airborne because they are missing an electron and are positively charged. The negative ion generator emits electrons, which are attracted to the positively odor molecules, bacteria, fungi, and other assorted dust floating in the air. Once the particles' charge is neutralized, they precipitate, fall to surfaces. Odor disappears and is replaced by grimy dust on surfaces.

While the grime may contain some odor molecules, it does not contain any appreciable amount of THC and also contains a lot of undesirable dust and pollutants.

The negative ions affect the odor molecules outside the glands so that the grow room becomes odorless. It is possible that they also penetrate the glands and deactivate the odor molecules. This is consistent with growers' observations that the buds lose their odor but not their potency in grow rooms with negative ion generators. They have found that the plants retain their odor when the ionizers are placed in the spaces surrounding the grow room.

SMELLY PROBLEM 11/96

I am growing in a 10' x 12' room using 1400 watts. I am using a Zestron ion fountain and a HEPA style air filter which circulates the air eight times an hour. My 480 cfm (cubic feet per minute) fan is wired to a thermostat-humidistat and is vented through air vents in the roof.

My house is tightly situated between two other homes, and there is heavy foot traffic across the street. Will the air filter and the ion fountain be effective in keeping the skunk aroma under wraps during the budding stage?

Big Daddy, Tacoma, WA

———

Odor is created in the grow room, but the problem begins when the smell migrates to other areas. This may seem obvious, but your system is designed to minimize the odor in the grow room and does not solve the problems outside that space.

Ion generators are inexpensive, use very little electricity, and are very effective. They work by loading the air with a negative electrical charge. Most odor particles are solids which are electrically charged because they are missing an electron. When the ions, loaded with an extra electron, and the electron deprived particles meet, the electron migrates to the particle. The particle is neutralized, it loses its odor and precipitates out of the air.

When ion generators are used in the grow-room they eliminate most of the odors but not the ones that leave the room. The generators also make the grass itself less odoriferous. The solution is to use the generators in the areas surrounding the grow-room including any out flow vents and doorway areas.

The HEPA filter eliminates bacteria and fungal spores as well as some odors that are airborne, so it should be kept in the grow space. Ozone generators, which create O_3, an unstable form of oxygen, are even more effective at eliminating odors

Clone & Seed Germination

LANKY GERMINATION 9/95

When my plants sprout they always grow too long and thin a stalk and bend over and die. What should I do to prevent this from happening?

DC, Las Cruces, NM

The seedlings are probably facing stress from three environmental conditions. First, they are probably not receiving adequate light. In naturalized stands the plants that are on the top of the canopy are usually the most successful. Their reaction is to stretch to reach more light. When plants receive adequate light, they grow shorter and stockier. Often plants started under a small fluorescent tube or near a not too bright window show these symptoms.

Second, the light may contain high levels in the red part of the light spectrum, which causes plants to grow tall. Incandescent and halogen bulbs, even "grow bulbs" all fit into this category. Stems grow longer under high pressure sodium lamps (HPS) than metal halides (MH) but this is usually not a problem.

Third, the plants may be too warm which causes stem elongation on many plants including cannabis. Temperatures should not go above the high seventies unless the plants have CO_2 enrichment. Then the thermometer can rise into the mid-eighties.

When transplanting, you may be tempted to bury a large part of the stem. This may be safe to do in relatively dry, fast draining soils, but it promotes stem rots in cool, damp mediums. A safer method of dealing with a weak stem is to stake it until it grows thicker. Ventilation which blows the plant around slightly helps strengthen the stem.

LIGHT FOR CUTTINGS 5/94

Dear Ed,

I took cuttings off my plants for cloning. I am keeping them in the same space as the mother and they are budding along with their "mother." How do I get them into vegetative growth?

Black Bart, Baltimore, MD

———

In order to grow vegetatively, cuttings need at least 18 hours of light a day. They could be lit continuously. Blue light promotes rooting. Cool white fluorescent tubes, which have a high proportion of blue light, might be the best for this purpose.

STORING CLONES 9/95

Can cuttings be taken and saved for later cloning? How long can they be stored? What are the best conditions?

J.D., Wichita, KS

———

A grower may wish to keep cuttings for a while before beginning the cloning process in order to coordinate timing with other stages.

This can be done easily by placing the clones in a container and keeping them in the refrigerator (not the freezer). The clones begin to lose their vigor after about seven days.

Take longer cuttings than usual. Then place them in a plastic bag which has been moistened by adding water and then draining. Seal the package and stick it in the fruit/vegetable section of the refrigerator. The clippings will be kept fresh in the same way as the vegetables.

When you are ready to use them, let them warm up to room temperature by removing them from the bag and letting them sit for about 15 minutes. Then clip off about $\frac{1}{2}$ inch from the cut end and follow normal cloning procedures. The cuttings are a little less viable, so there may be a small increase in losses.

After about ten days in the cooler, the cuttings begin to lose energy and rot, and viability declines quickly.

Another way to store clones is to root them and then keep them in a cool environment, under low light conditions (15 watts fluorescent) with a weak fertilizer solution (300 ppm, 2-5-3). They can hang out for several months this way.

REGENERATION 1/94

Dear Ed,

How is regeneration done? Can you put a bare stem into a continuous light regimen and have it regrow?

QP, U.S.A.

Some bud material and leaf should be left on the plant during harvest. Completely stripped plants will not regnerate. The plant is placed under continuous light and fed a high nitgoghen fertilizer formula. The plant begins regeneration from leaf/bud material.

General Growing—Plants

MICROWAVED WATER 6/94

Dear Ed,

I am growing in an attic and it gets pretty cold up there. The temperature, with the lights off, goes down to 55 degrees. Can I microwave the water to warm it before using it to water the plants?

Captain Cloud, Kamloops, B.C., Canada

Yes. Heated Water (to 72 to 75 degrees F) will prevent any shock to the roots.

CO_2 AT NIGHT 2/92

Dear Ed,

During the daylight hours plants use CO_2 and expel O_2, and at night the process is reversed. O_2 is used and CO_2 is expelled. With this in mind, should the CO_2 tank be turned off during the dark photoperiod of the flowering cycle?

Leca, Adelphi, MD

———

Yes. There is no reason to keep the CO_2 levels elevated during the dark period.

TOO MUCH CO_2 9/94

Dear Ed,

Can a plant be given too much CO_2? Can seltzer water be used to supply the plants with the gas? Do you think it can enhance potency?

Green & Organic Frogs, Manasota, FL

———

Usually growers give plants between 1000 and 1500 parts per million (PPM) CO_2. In especially well lit gardens the plants can use up to 2000 PPM. Plant leaves start to exhibit CO_2 burn at between 2000 and 2500 PPM.

Seltzer water contains only water and CO_2. It can be used to supply the gas to the plants. It is not really an efficient way to supply it except when the plants are small. Once they get large they require a large quantity to spray the plants several times a day. In order to get the water to spread evenly over the plants use a commercial wetting agent or a $\frac{1}{4}$ teaspoon of detergent per quart of seltzer. Do not use club soda. It has salt added and is not good for the plants.

CO_2 does not enhance potency. It increases the growth rate by speeding up photosynthesis when the plant is given adequate light, water, and nutrients. The time spent in vegetative cycle is decreased and flowering is speeded up. The plant tissue also grows thicker.

Some growers think that CO_2 treatment should be eliminated during the last two weeks of flowering. They claim that it decreases potency when used as the flower enters final ripening.

HORIZONTAL GROWING

Dear Ed,

Is it possible to grow a plant horizontally in a dresser drawer?

T.D., Tyrone, PA

It is much easier to grow marijuana vertically rather than horizontally. But, it can be done. Marijuana is subject to phototropism in response to light. This makes plants grow towards light. Geotropism, in response to gravity, makes plants grow vertically.

Fluorescent tubes are placed along the sides of the drawer, and in the center if the drawer is deep enough. The plants will grow somewhat towards the light rather than vertically, and the geotropism will be somewhat controlled. Either wire mesh or wooden stakes should be set up either on top or under the plants. As they grow they are tied down with wire twists. Another way to control the growth is by placing the plants inside wire mesh tubes for better control.

The drawer should be vented from the back using several mini-fans pushing air in from holes near the bottom and out from holes in the top. The best way to vent when the area is secure from prying eyes is to open the drawer. This will solve the CO_2 problem, too.

Even when closed, light will probably seep out so it is best to turn the system off when company is expected. The chest should also be placed in a space where guests are not expected to open the drawer. Explaining the magical metamorphosis of a sock drawer to garden requires a lot of creativity. (When I left this morning I did note that the socks were lit very brightly...)

A custom designed container to accommodate the horizontal stalk is needed, or the stalk could be creased, that is, turned 90° until the stem creases. It may have to be supported after that.

Will it work? As long as the plants are kept trained and the heat is dispersed, yes.

REMOVE SHADE LEAVES? 5/94

Dear Ed,

Are you supposed to remove the shade leaves? What happens if you remove too many?

Baffled, Blasdell, NY

You can consider each shade leaf as a tiny factory which uses the energy from red and blue light to combine the hydrogen (H) from water (H_2O) with CO_2 to create the basic building block of most life on earth, CH_2O, sugar.[1]

Sugar is used by the plant for several purposes. Some of it is combined with nitrogen (N) to form amino acids. The rest is either stored as carbohydrate or used to fuel metabolism.

When you remove a shade leaf, you are eliminating a source of sugar to the plant. The leaves should only be removed for specific purposes. Leaves at the bottom of the plant receive little light and prevent air circulation. They are often trimmed off to increase air flow. Leaves which are shading a growing bud can also be removed. This allows more light to the leaves at the site of the developing bud, increasing its growth rate.

TRIM FAN LEAVES? 3/92

Dear Ed,

I am growing a few plants in a small space. I have been pruning the large fan leaves from the nodes on the main stems because:

• It prevents shading of new growth.

• It allows the plant to put all its energy into growing these new branches. More branches equals more nodes, which means more buds.

• The leaves are rather potent and provide a tolerable smoke until harvest time.

Are any of these assumptions mistaken? Am I harming my crop?

Albert, Buffalo, NY———

Although the fan leaves shade the new tissue, they also provide the energy it needs for growth. Rather than being an energy drain, the fan leaves require little energy for the plant to run, since they are mature and not growing. Instead, they function as factories producing sugar.

By removing the leaves, a source of energy is removed from the plant. However, in a limited space, and with light from a single point source, rather than the ambient light found in a sunlit area, the shade leaves may never allow new growth to come in contact with the light, so their removal sometimes helps the plant grow.

Although more branches mean more bud sites, the total weight of buds in a given growing space is often higher when plants are pruned, limiting the total number of branches. Then the plant puts more of its

---

1. The exact formula is $CO2 = 2H20 = (CH2) + H2O + O2$

energy into each remaining branch, resulting in a few large, heavy buds rather than masses of rather small ones.

Removing bottom branches and leaves, which receive little light, also helps focus plant energy on upper limb growth.

GREEN MEDIUM 2/93

Dear Ed,
Why does my medium consisting of vermiculite and perlite turn green?
Paranoid Puffs, Columbus, Ohio

———

The medium is an ideal environment for algae to grow. It is moist, has access to air and light, and contains nutrients. The algae, which use some nutrients, are often considered a nuisance. To eliminate them, place a piece of reflective material or a layer of gravel on top so that the surface stays dry and dark.

REMOVING LOWER LEAVES 2/93

Dear Ed,
Does removing the lower branches affect the plant?
J. Doobie

———

Larger plants often have vegetation continually hidden in shadow. These lower branches receive virtually no energy and are not productive. Removing them increases air circulation which is especially important in a closed environment. It also forces plants to put more energy into the larger branches.

THREE LEAVES 6/94

Dear Ed,
I have a female plant which has three leaves rather than two at each joint. If I pollinate it with a male which had only two leaves, would any of the resulting seed produce plants with three branches?
Clandestine Grower, Oroville, CA

———

Probably not in the first generation (F1) hybrids. The allele (version of a gene) for three leaves is recessive so that all of the plants will have two leaves. However, crosses between the F1 hybrids result in plants that have alleles from the two parents mixed randomly. The plants' characteristics differentiate out so that there is considerable variance. Some plants will have two alleles for three leaves and exhibit that characteristic. A better way to create 3 leaved plants would be to take clones, reverse sex on some and then make the cross.

SMELLY WATER 9/92

Dear Ed,

When watering my pot plants I always leach about 20%. When this overflow of water is real yellow and/or smelly, what does this mean? Would it be bad to water my other house plants with this? I use a very rich soil.

S & M, Boston, Massachusetts

It means there is anaerobic decomposition taking place. This is an indication that the soil is too dense and holding so much water that no air can get to the roots. Roots need oxygen to stay healthy. This crop the problem can be resolved by watering less frequently, allowing the soil to dry a little, thus letting the soil absorb air.

In the future add substances to the mix that allow better drainage. They include sand, pebbles, perlite and vermiculite.

RE-USING POTTING MIX 3/97

I use a soilless mix composed of 50% perlite, 25% vermiculite, 15% peat moss and 10% sand. I add a time release fertilizer and fertilize the 3 gallon containers with dilute mixes of organic and synthetic fertilizers. The plants are rootbound when they are harvested at 3 months.

Would I be better off buying new constituents? What would I need to do to re-use the mix?

Gingerbread Man, Kansas

I think that re-using the mix is asking for trouble. Any infections which the plants may have would be transferred to the new plants. If the soil is prepared in bulk, any infection that a single plant may have contracted, could be transferred to all of the new plants.

When you think of how much each container yields, and the small cost of the potting mix, it seems inappropriate to go through all the effort and introducing risk for the sake of saving a few dollars.

There are three solutions to your desire to re-use your mix. First, you could change from your mix to hydro-clay, the clay pellets which absorb water and can be used in many kinds of hydro systems including such low effort units as wick and reservoir systems. They are easily cleaned, can actually be washed with detergent, and are sterilized using a water-hydrogen peroxide solution. The pellets are a permanent medium. They never have to be replaced. I have some that I have used for different houseplants and vegetables, for twenty years.

Second, the plants could be pruned and regenerated. To do this, leave some vegetation on the branches which you wish to keep, and remove the other branches. Once the plants regrow, in 5 -30 days, place them back into flowering. They will grow a whole new harvest and the mix has been re-used with no effort.

Third, the potting mix can be re-used, profitably. Mix it with your garden soil, use it for raised beds, planting boxes, and containers, or mix it into your raw compost. Almost all infections in the mix are probably specific to cannabis or inactive under outdoor conditions.

Hydro

ALGAE IN WATER 6/94

Dear Ed,

I use a wick system. I can't keep algae from growing in the water. Any suggestions?

J., Hickory, NC

———

The algae need light in order to grow. Keep the reservoir covered so no light gets to it. Covering the top of the plant containers and reservoir with opaque material such as black plastic will prevent their growth.

ALGAE IN HYDRO SYSTEM 6/96

In the clay medium and nutrient tank in my hydro system there is always algae growing. How can I eliminate this?

X-Ray, OR

_____

The algae need light and moisture to grow. Since you cannot deprive them of moisture, you must eliminate sources of light such as light transmitting tubing, tanks and containers. One way to do this is to cover the hydro area with reflective material which bounces the light back up to the plants rather than letting it penetrate to the root area. Some people make collars out of mylar or aluminum foil to prevent light getting to the planting medium.

One grower solved the problem using a UVC lamp kit from an aquarium shop. This light kit is designed expressly for this purpose. The hydro water remained clear and clog-free even without covers on the top of his rockwool.

However, another grower told me he thought the light broke down the nutrients in the solution.

ORGANIC HYDROPONICS

Can I make a good organic hydroponic solution from liquid tea guanos and seaweeds?

As I create my recipe for a complete fertilizer do I just add the numbers together?

Crystal River Buds, Dunnellon, FL

_____

It is possible to make an organic hydroponic fertilizer solution. Guano and seaweed teas are good ingredients.

There are various guanos available offering several different N-P-K ratios. In addition, a kelp fertilizer will help with micro-nutrients. You should also consider using composted chicken or poultry manure.

The easiest way to use these ingredients is to brew a tea by letting the ingredients steep in a plastic container. The nutrients will dissolve in the water over a day or two. Hot water helps the solids dissolve.

In order to have any idea of what is happening with the solution, an EC or electrical conductivity meter, is required. Its reading corresponds to the parts per million (ppm) of dissolved solids (nutrients) in the water. This tea can be used as a fertilizing solution for biohydroponics.

Plants can be foliar fed, too, bypassing the root system. Dilute solutions of filtered organic teas can be sprayed directly on the leaves. The best time to do this is during the lighted part of the cycle so that the water dries fairly quickly.

BAT GUANO TEA FOR HYDRO 6/96

I read an article on using bat guano in a tea type solution for hydroponic systems. He said that he put the guano into a coffee or tea bag and let it steep for two days and that he had gotten good results. I have a home-built hydroponic system and I tried it. After two days the water was only slightly discolored. I tested it with my TDS meter (total dissolved solids) and it tested at only 350 ppm (parts per million). The tap water tested at 120 ppm.

To concentrate the nutrient I decided to use a percolator type coffee pot. In just a minute it started to brew the "guano java." A dark liquid came out. After it cooled it tested at 1700 ppm, a much better result. Then I changed the water several times but used the same guano, which resulted in a slightly lower ppm each time. I put the residue in a soil mixture.

Pot Protester, PA

———

Thanks for the brewing tip, Pot.

WATER RESERVOIR 6/94 (WATER FOUNTAIN)

Dear Ed,

I saw that Liz was using "water fountains" to hold extra water in her reservoir. Could you tell me how to make one?

Scarlet Begonia, Toledo, OH

———

Liz bought the "water fountain" at a supermarket during Christmas season, 1987. Since that time I have not seen them for sale. They were designed to maintain water level without constant refilling of the tree holder. They were manufactured by Molor Products, address unknown. Each fountain holds a 2 liter soda pop bottle. The device, which works totally passively, without any moving parts, maintains a two inch water level.

From the picture you can see how the device works. The water is held in the bottle because a vacuum would be created if it flowed out. Only when the water level in the tray being filled goes below the fountains's level, can air get into the bottle which releases water and refills the tray. These can be built to hold larger containers.

Additives

OZONE

Dear Ed,

I have two closet gardens. I use ozone in one of them. It does remarkably well. No moldy fuzz grows. My other garden must be sprayed with hydrogen peroxide every few days.

Leaves are larger and healthier and drop off is practically nil. Growth rate is about 20% faster, but not as good as spraying seltzer. Then I switched the machine to the other space. The plants there are doing much better and the other closet is losing leaves from yellowing.

The ozone machine does not have much effect on gnats and only a partial success with white flies. It wiped out my spiders, lady beetles and praying mantis. Aphids are also controlled.

Don, Downey, CA

Thanks for your report, Don. Anyone else using an ozone machine? Reports please.

STYROFOAMED SOIL

Dear Ed,

When growing in containers I make a bottom layer of soil consisting of styrofoam chips mixed with planting medium, worm castings and vermiculite. It helps drainage and lets the roots really breathe. The plants always respond well. Does anything leach out from the foam?

D. A. P., NYC, NY

Styrofoam chips are an excellent additive to planting mixes. They are light weight and hydrophobic (they repel water). As you said, this allows the roots to breathe by physically removing water from spaces in the soil mix so that air pockets form.

There have been reports that in the presence of acidic drinks such as coffee, there is some breakdown of the foam. The presence of various salts may accelerate the speed of decomposition. Even so, I think that styrofoam is safe to use and does not pose a threat. The processes for manufacturing it are another matter.

SUGAR JUNKIE

Dear Ed,

I tried feeding my plants with a needle and thread dipped into flavoring which was then run through the stem of the plant. I tried sugar using the same method and had controls to compare. The plant I experimented with was the smallest of the 30 day old plants, about 2 inches shorter with less development. In four days the plant reached the height of the others. The only problem was that the corn syrup-water solution kept crystallizing on the thread, which was a real pain.

Is it possible to inject the plants with a similar solution using a hypodermic needle?

Ludwig, GA

Yes it is. The solution can be injected in minute quantities. Giant vegetable growers sometimes inject their plants in order to get their vegetables to grow larger.

SUPERTHRIVE EXPERIMENT

Dear Ed,

In the "Best of High Times #12" there is an article titled "Goin' For Growth" by Bob Ireland. In that article, Bob mentions several products that contain hormones that may help cause plants to become female. I tried "Superthrive."

I grew two crops from the same batch of seeds. It was a fine purple indica that has been growing in the Hudson River Valley for over ten years. I grew one crop with Superthrive, the control without.

The crop that was grown with it showed males at six weeks at 18 hours of light. Out of 60 plants, 12, or 20% were male. The females did not show sex until light was reduced to 12 hours.

The control was grown identically to the first except I did not use Superthrive. Out of 60 plants I got 39 males and they did not sex early.

The quality of the buds was excellent from both crops except the buds from the first crop were slightly better and more numerous.

Harvey Hemp, Fishkill, NY

———

Great experiment. Thanks for reporting the results Mr. Hemp.

SUPERTHRIVE II

Harvey Hemp's letter discussed how he had earlier sexing and more males when he used Superthrive. Usually it is used for plants which have suffered root damage. It replenishes the damaged area with to instantly available vitamins and hormones, rather than waiting for the plant to produce them itself. This reduces repair time.

Superthrive can be used in hydroponic systems at the rate of one drop per gallon during vegetative cycle, but should be discontinued before flowering.

I have also used Spray-N-Grow, which is a micronutrient complex that acts as a bio-catalyst. Bloom weight typically doubles.

These supplements and others are carried by Eco Enterprises, 800-426-6937

The Plant Doctor, Rayland, OH

———

Thanks for the info Mr. Doctor. Has anyone else tried these experiments? Perhaps we can get a real controlled tests going.

SPRAY-N-GROW

Dear Ed,

I experimented with a product called "Spray-N-Grow." It is all natural and can be sprayed on the plant up to the day of harvest. It is advertised to dramatically increase weight and yield of tomatoes and other vegetables. Bottom line: it works on cannabis, too.

The plants treated with Spray-N-Grow produced huge, dense, heavy buds. The dried buds are rock hard and have a pleasant, fruity flavor.

I highly recommend that you seek out this product. It really works.

D.K.B., Sheridan, OR

———

Thanks for the letter, D. Other correspondents have recommended this product, too. It is made from natural plant hormones and is certified as totally safe for all edibles.

It is available from:

Spray-N-Grow, P.O.B. 2137, Rockport, TX 78381
Tel. 512-790-9033, Fax. 512-790-9313

The company also makes "Triple Action 20" which is a fungicide, algicide, and bactericide spray that prevents fungi and molds on plants. It is classified by the EPA as safe for ornamentals, but it breaks down in 1-50 hours and has been used safely on edibles.

Pests & Disease

SPIDER MITE RELIEF 5/94

Dear Ed,

I recently harvested a crop which became infected during flowering. By carefully removing heavily populated sun leaves, I held them at bay until harvest. When drying I found that when I draped plastic wrap over the buds on the line, the mites gathered at the top as they instinctively seek the high ground. I kept changing the plastic until the buds were dry. Would loosely draped plastic wrap or sticky paper on the tops of growing buds trap the mites?

Still Learning, Queens, NY

———

Yes. The mites will climb off the plants and can be trapped.

BACTERIA AND VIRUSES 4/97

I've been an indoor grower for 7 years and started experiencing nutrient uptake problems about 2 years ago. I think that a virus or bacteria is my problem.

What strategies can I use to eliminate the problem? Does bleach kill the virus? How do these infections spread, through the water or air?

John, Dayton, OH

———

Bacteria and viruses spread in several ways. Some are air or water borne organisms, others use plant pests as vectors. Some may spread by physical contact with other plants (including roots) or animals. Once the micro-organisms are in a garden, they spread through the growing medium or recirculated water. In contact with a suitable environment they multiply quickly.

I suspect that many changes in the characteristics reported by growers are the result of infections. These include reduced odor and yields, lowered potency, and problems with nutrient uptake.

Plants do not have the immune systems found in animals so they are not able to fight infections. Typical responses of plants are to isolate the infection by growing tissue around it, planned death of infected parts and seed production. Viruses and bacteria are much less likely to infect seed than other plant parts, so the next crop starts off uninfected.

This means that there is no cure for an infected garden or its plants. To be rid of the infection the plants must be destroyed. The garden must be thoroughly cleaned. All walls and floors should be wiped down with a hydrogen peroxide or vinegar solution. All instruments and tools should be thoroughly washed or boiled. The planting medium or substrate should be discarded. All tables, containers, trays, lines, and pumps should be thoroughly washed, wiped, and flushed with sterilizing solution, i.e., hydrogen peroxide bleach or detergent.

As I mentioned earlier, seeds are usually free of infection. Another plant part usually infection free is the meristem growing tip. The tiny growing tips are often used for tissue culture cloning, starting with a few cells.

There are several ways to lessen the chance of garden infection:
1. Filter all air coming into the room. This also lessens the chance of insect or pest infection. Mites, aphids and other pests sometimes ride on air currents.
2. Don't go into the indoor garden after working or brushing through plants outside. Infections can hitch a ride on you or your clothing.

3.   Recirculating water is a master vector for infection. A UVC filter for
     the water would destroy many pathogens. UVC filters are manufac-
     tured for aquarium specialists and are easily fitted into recirculating
     systems.
4.   Never introduce a clone into your system without isolating it several
     months from infection. Many growers have had gardens ticking
     along until they introduced a clone holding a pest or infection. In one
     case, Walter Reed style, a grower introduced to his garden a single
     clone with a known nutrient uptake disorder. Within months the
     space had to be sterilized. In another case, a grower was given
     clones, from a great variety, which were infected with mites. He kept
     them isolated in a separate room as he rooted them and tried to elim-
     inate the mites. The mites spread to the main room and were eventu-
     ally eliminated using a combination of sprays, isolation and thor-
     ough hygiene.

KILLING MITES 4/97

I found a great way to kill mites on clones and small plants. I add
two heaping tablespoons of cornstarch per cup of water and dip the clones
or spray the plants paying particular attention to the undersides of the
leaves and also the top of the growing medium. The water evaporates
quickly leaving the cornstarch to dry and mummify the suckers. If you
spray the plants daily for three weeks you will be rid of the pests.

                                        Harriet T. Hempster Lansing, MI

––––––

Good idea for clones and other small plants, Harriet. I would add
just a dash of detergent to spread the water quickly. Also, you could make
a "tea" by pouring a cup of boiling water over a couple of mashed garlic
cloves, a tablespoon of mashed raw onion and a tablespoon of mixed
Italian seasoning. Mix this tea with the cornstarch and detergent, for an
even more powerful general pesticide.

Flowering

POWER OUTAGE 12/93

Dear Ed,

Does a power outage during a blooming light cycle seriously affect the plants?

The Lone Coyote, Shreveport, LA

———

An occasional power outage during the blooming cycle will not seriously affect the plants.

Cannabis plants flower in response to a dark period of about 12 hours or more. If the light is blocked for a while, the plant's dark cycle is not affected. The light must go back on during the regular light cycle only, which should remain unchanged.

LIGHT INTERRUPTION 4/94

Dear Ed,

My garden is in a closet. I have to turn the plants' light off occasionally when people come over. Does that harm the plants? The lights are off for half an hour every few days.

Steve, Eaton, IN

———

The slight interruption in lighting will have a negligible effect upon the plants. During the interruption they will stop photosynthesizing but the few hours of light lost each week will not be noticeable.

VISION DURING THE DARK PERIOD 3/97

Let's say you have to go into the grow room during the dark period. You turn on the lights. Do you then reset the lights to 12 hours of darkness?

Making Ends Meet, Humboldt, CA

———

Rather than turn on the lights, use a flashlight with a green filter over it. Plants are insensitive to green light so they will not be affected. You can enter the room without disturbing them.

If the lights are turned on once, the accident will not have much effect on the buds. If it happenes repeatedly it will delay ripening and cause running buds.

SORTING MALES PRE-FLOWERING 11/92

Dear Ed,

I may have stumbled upon a shortcut for thinning a crop of seedlings for both sex and quality. When the seedlings are about four weeks plants whose tops are not stinky are destroyed. This eliminates most males and many females of poor quality. It saves space and effort.

I discovered this trick while raising, sexing, flowering and testing 37 seedlings taken from separate high quality stash purchases. The plants were raised under a metal halide (MH) lamp. I noticed that some tops smelled and some didn't. At four weeks, the aroma of all tops was recorded as follows: stinky-6 plants, faint stinky-2, green smell-2, no smell-27. All were later forced to flower. Males and hermaphrodites were removed as they were identified. The females were all grown to maturity and smoke tested. All five finalists had smelled stinky. The remaining stinky was a male. The two faint stinkies were an inferior female and a hermaphrodite. Of the 27 with no smell, 8 were males, 18 inferior females and 1 hermaphrodite.

Midnite Sharecropper, Lexington, KY

MALE FLOWERING 10/95

I am running the lights continuously in my grow room. All of my plants are healthy. the thing that baffles me is that one of the plants is developing male flowers. Is this common? Why is it showing sex under vegetative regimen?

Baffled, Denver, CO

With most varieties, female marijuana plants use a light regimen to determine when they go from vegetative to flowering growth. Male plants also use this and flower if they receive a regular regimen of long periods of uninterrupted darkness. However, unlike the females of most varieties, males tend to flower as they get older regardless of the light regimen.

READY TO FLOWER? 4/94

Dear Ed,

How can you tell when the plants are ready to be forced to flower? When should I switch to a flowering fertilizer?

Etu, Tampa, FL

As the number of hours of uninterrupted darkness increases the plants start to flower. Plants can be forced to flower at any time. Indoors, they flower when given 12 hours of uninterrupted darkness each 24 hour cycle.

The plants should be forced at your convenience. The flowering should coincide with your schedule and the plants should be forced at a convenient size before they get too large or too crowded. Once they are forced, they will grow an additional 20–50% in height. Some sativas will grow even more.

Generally, once the plants are 18 inches tall additional height will not increase total yield since little light penetrates beyond the canopy.

EXTREME FLOWER FORCING 5/96

I started my plants on a 24 hour cycle. After a month, I switched it to 10 hours on, 14 hours off. The buds are small. How can I make them bigger?

Help Wanted, Bobtown, MA

The reason that the buds are small is the lighting cycle. Marijuana flowers when the uninterrupted dark period reaches 12 hours each evening. With fewer hours of darkness, the flowering is likely to be somewhat ambiguous, with some flowering, but continued vegetative growth. With more hours of darkness, the buds ripen more quickly, but their growth time is shortened, and they reach maturity without growing to full size.

The buds on your plants would have grown larger if they had been given a light regimen of 12 on, 12 off.

PLANTS NOT FLOWERING 3/92

Dear Ed,

I am growing some plants under three 150 watt "Gro-N-Sho" bulbs in a 3½' x 3½' x 6' grow space covered with reflective surfaces. The plants were all grown together under the same conditions on using a regimen of 16 hours of light, eight hours of darkness each day. I triggered the plants to flower by turning the light cycle back to 12 hours each of light and darkness. It is now three weeks later and one plant is blooming like crazy and the other four aren't even showing sex. What's happening?

K-N-D, MD

There are two possibilities. One is that the plants are different varieties. Some plants mature earlier than others. Late maturing plants such as equatorials often take several weeks longer than indoor adapted varieties to indicate. Even so, you may notice a few signs of the change from vegetative to flowering. Vegetative growth slows and then stops, and then the first flowers appear at the node, where the leaves join the branch at the third or fourth leaf from the top. Using a photographer's loupe or a magnifying glass, the primordial flower's sex can sometimes be determined. Some equatorial varieties require 13 or 14 hours of darkness per day in order to flower profusely.

Another possibility is light pollution. The plants are sensitive to even dim lights. If the darkness is not complete, but light leaks into the garden, some plants will remain in vegetative state. Another problem could be that the lights are turned on momentarily during the dark period, interrupting the cycle. Once a light is turned on, the countdown of number of hours of uninterrupted darkness restarts. Varieties vary in their tolerance of light pollution.

RIPENING BUDS 12/93

Dear Ed,

What can I do to hasten the ripening of my buds? I've already shortened the light cycle to 14 hours of darkness instead of 12. My plants are a hybrid and they are short and stalky, but they've been flowering continuously for over two months. How can I get them into rapid ripening?

I am growing in rockwool using an ebb and flow system. Do I dare stop fertilizing when growing in water?

D.K., MN

Your plants have only been flowering for 55 days. Most varieties take 70 days or more to flower, in spite of seed catalog claims of 55–60 days or 6–8 weeks. Those are exaggerations. Your plants will probably ripen in 2–3 weeks. However, some varieties seem to have a more definitive ripening time than others indoors. Although virtually all varieties can be induced to flower indoors under a regimen of twelve hours of uninterrupted darkness each day, ripening is a different matter. Indica varieties ripen within 70 to 80 days of flower induction. The pistils wither and begin to withdraw into the false seed pods which swell. The glands fill with resin and THC and new growth slows.

Water stress induces earlier ripening in outdoor plants. However, its applicability to indoor growing techniques, especially hydroponics, is questionable. In hydroponic systems, the line between water stress and tissue damage is a thin one.

Pollinating the entire crop may be a better method of ripening recalcitrant flowers. If pollen were released after the buds filled out, each flower would start to produce seed. The pistil would recede into the calyx and seed formation would begin. If the buds were picked seven to ten days after pollination, they would appear ripened.

BLACK LIGHT 2/93

Dear Ed,

I've found that using a black light during the 12 hour dark cycle creates thicker, bigger buds. I have a 3' x 4' closet garden with 3 plants in it. I use three one hundred watt incandescent black light bulbs. That gives each square foot two 25 watts of black light. When I used 5 bulbs I got lankier, smaller buds. Why is this?

Growing Black, Colonia, NJ

———

Thanks for the research Mr. Black. Perhaps the plants were getting too hot.

CO_2 AT RIPENING 5/96

Why do people reduce the use of CO_2 during the last two weeks of ripening?

Professor Afghani, Staten Island, NY

———

Some growers claim that the odor and the potency are reduced with CO_2 during the last stages of flowering.

Morphological changes are apparent in CO_2 treated plants; the leaves and stems are thicker, the color is often darker, and sativa leaves often become squatter, looking more like afghanis. The stomata are also affected. I have not seen any studies describing changes in the odor or taste of herbs or flowers and have not noticed differences, myself. Since the growth of new tissue slows as the flowers ripen, the CO_2 loses much of its effectiveness then, so it is shut off.

HERMAPHRODITE FLOWERS

Dear Ed,

Suppose you have a potent strain which you wish to perpetuate. If the plant grows a few male flowers as it ripens, would the seed be genetically identical to the mother plant? Will all my seed from this be female?

Indoor Indica, New Castle, DE

———

The seed would be close to the mother plant but not identical. The reason is that with sexual reproduction there are millions of possible combinations of genes. The seeds will all have genes from the same plant however, so all of the combinations will show most of the mother plant's characteristics. Cannabis has five pair or ten chromosomes. Each gene, which affects or represents a characteristic, is represented twice on each pair of chromosomes. When the pollen or ovum is formed, the pairs of chromosomes split and only one half of each pair is contained in each reproductive cell. The chromosomes split in a seemingly random manner, so that there are billions of combinations possible.

For each gene, there are only two choices, so there is a 50% chance that the plant will have the same combination as the mother if the mother has two different forms of the same gene, and there is a 50% chance that the resulting plant will have a pair of genes which are alike.

When the plant is hermaphroditic early in the season, about half of the seed produced from it will be female and half hermaphroditic. If the plant turns hermaphroditic late in the season there is a chance that it is the result of environmental stress or a ripening phenomenon. Seeds resulting from this pollen may be all female.

SAVING POLLEN 5/93

Dear Ed,

We are currently growing a Northern Lights (NL) plant which turned out to be a male. We decided to let it grow anyway in order to pollinate a female to get some seeds.The problem is, our only female is not a NL and we wanted to preserve the pure strain. Can we preserve the pollen until we get a female?

R.A.G.S., Cincinnati, OH

————

The pollen can be preserved for several weeks in the refrigerator in a sealed container containing a desiccant such as silica gel or rice flour. Pollen can also be frozen in a sealed container with desiccant for a period of at least one year and remain viable.

STORING POLLEN 1/97

What is the correct way to collect and store pollen? How long can it be stored?

S.J., Tampa, FL

————

Remove the plant or branch from the garden. Branches can be placed in water containing a dilute nutrient solution. When the flowers are about to open, place the branch on a piece of paper in a draft free area. The flowers will open, releasing the pollen, which will fall onto the paper. After the flowers have opened, tap the branches to remove any remaining pollen. Place the pollen in a 35mm film can or other small container. Put a desiccant pack in the pack, cover it and place in the refrigerator. The pollen will remain viable for several weeks. Stored in the freezer, it will stay viable for long periods.

STORING SEEDS AND POLLEN 6/94

Dear Ed,

How should I store seeds for long periods of time. Would vacuum sealing work?

Harold Hedge Bender, Minneapolis, MN

————

They can be vacuum packed and stored in the freezer. A desiccator, which draws moisture from the air should be included, since moisture is injurious to seeds.

MIXING POLLEN 7/92

Dear Ed,
If pollen from several varieties is mixed together, will each pistil pick just one grain or will the resulting seed be a mix? What will happen if two pistils from the same plant are fertilized with pollen from different varieties?

T.H.C., Bangor, ME

———

Each pistil accepts only one pollen grain. The resulting seed is of genetic material from one male and one female.

When two pistils from the same plant are fertilized with pollen from different plants, each seed will contain the female's genetic information and the genetic information from the male which fertilized it.

The Smoke

POT WON'T BURN 5/94

Dear Ed,
I recently harvested my first small indoor crop. My problem is that the dried buds will not stay lit, which makes it impossible to roll the pot into joints because it crystallizes into this black substance.

I read in a previous column of yours that this might be caused by a lack of potassium. I have tried various drying methods and none produced pot that will stay lit. These included microwaving, sun drying for 1–2 days, and slow drying hanging upside down.

If the problem does indicate a lack of K, how and when should the nutrient be added?

My second question is that I am stuck with $\frac{1}{2}$ lb. of good looking and smelling pot which won't burn. Is there any way I can fix these buds?

Useless Green, Tallahassee, FL

———

The black substance is carbon (C), which is what is left once the other substances have boiled or evaporated or burned. C by itself does not burn with a high enough heat to keep the fire going. When combined with K there is a higher burn temperature and the burn stays lit.

When wood or charcoal is burned, the ash which remains is mostly potash, K_2O. In order to get a satisfactory marijuana, the fertilizer regimen should be changed. The plants should be fed a fertilizer with a higher ratio of phosphorous (P) such as 4-3-5 during the first few weeks of growth. This will help the plants develop short, stocky stems rather than thinner, taller growth.

During the last three weeks of flowering the fertilizer ratio should be low in N, high in P, and medium in K—between 1-5-3 and 3-7-5, (This stands for the ratio of N-P-K, always in that order.) or their multiples. This encourages flowering, and causes a nitrogen (N) deficiency. The plant transfers N from its old growth, the shade leaves, to the new growth, flowers and the small leaves surrounding them. The shade leaves turn yellow and die as the N migrates to the new tissue.

Your non joint burning marijuana may be a blessing in disguise. Instead of smoking in a joint, use a small bowl water-pipe or use for cooking.

You will get a much cleaner smoke since you are not smoking paper. The C of your K deficient pot does not burn, and the smoke is filtered of water solubles through water. Why would anyone want all that C or its pyrolitic, carbon monoxide (CO), which is considered a poison and CO_2 in her/his lungs? Another benefit is that a pipe is a much more efficient way to get high than a joint. Much less material is wasted as sidestream smoke in an efficient pipe.

Chapter Thirty–Four
Experiments

Horticulturists have reported a number of methods for increasing plant yeilds which are still in the experimental stage. These include stimulating growth using an electrical current, the use of estrogen and progestin, and the use of strobe lighting.

ELECTRICITY

Experiments at the University of Maryland indicate that a very weak electrical current running through the soil increases the growth rates of plants. This stimulation seems to be most effective when the plants are not receiving a lower than optimum level of light. Some researchers speculate that the current increases the roots' efficiency in obtaining nutrients by affecting the chemical-electrical charges of the nutrient dissolved in the water. One company manufactures a photovoltaic device specifically to charge the soil. The magazine *Mother Earth News* reported in the March 1984 issue that plant growth can be doubled using these devices.

"Sun Stiks" are available from Silicon Sensors, Highway 18 East, Dodgeville, Wisconsin 53533.

FEMALE HORMONES — BIRTH CONTROL PILLS

Over the years there have been a lot of anecdotal reports indicating that birth control pills stimulate plant growth. In 1983, a farmer in Texas reported that his tomato plants grew many more tomatoes after they received two treatments with estrogen-based pills.

There may be a problem of safety regarding the use of these hormones. There have been no studies on what happens to the hormone once it is taken up by the plant. When estrogen is given to farm animals, it increases their growth rate, but the meat contains traces of the substance, which sometimes affects people who eat it.

STROBE LIGHTS

Some botanists have speculated that the pigments which are used in photosynthesis respond to energy peaks in the light wave. These scientists believe that much of the light is wasted by the plant because it isn't "peak". They speculate that much energy could be saved by supplying the plant only with light "peaks". One way to do this is by using a strobe unit in place of conventional lighting. The strobe flashes a high intensity of light, but it is on for only fractions of a second. The result is that the plants receive many light peaks in between periods of darkness.

There has been little research on this theory, but one grower claimed to get satisfactory results.

One way to use a strobe without too much risk might be to use it to supplement more conventional lighting. If a higher growth rate is noticed, the strobes could be tried alone. Should this system work, electrical costs could be lowered by as much as 75%.

A Letter to Readers

I gathered the information in this book from primary research as well as through interviews and correspondence with growers. I appreciate this contact and will continue to try and make myself available to individuals with similar interests.

Your ideas, criticisms, feedback and comments help to shape future works. They are invaluable to my research activities. Newspaper articles about growing, eradication activities, and other topics of interest are also helpful. Finally, any research material including university studies and scientific articles help to round out the information cycle.

I already receive quite a bit of mail about marijuana and its cultivation, and I do not have the time to answer it all personally. However, I do read it all. I currently write a column for *High Times* magazine called "Ask Ed" in which I answer readers' questions about marijuana; your question may very well be answered in that column or in other articles in *High Times* or *Sinsemilla Tips*.

You have a better chance of receiving an answer if you enclose a self-addressed, stamped envelope, but still, there are no guarantees. Any correspondence suggesting my participation or encouragement of an illegal activity will be ignored.

Stay high,

Ed Rosenthal
High Times
211 East 43rd Street
New York, New York 10017

The following companies contributed photographs to this book:

Dutch Passion
P.O. Box 1579
1000 B.N
Amsterdam

Paradise Seeds
P.O. Box 377
1000 AJ
Amsterdam
Holland

Marc Emery Seeds
P.O. Box 69
307 West Hastings Street
Vancouver, BC
Canada
V6B 1H4
http://hempbc.com

Sagarmartha Seeds
Lijnbaansgracht 90
1015 GZ
Amsterdam
Holland
http://www.xs4all/~seeds

Green House Seed Co.
P.O. Box 75162
1076 ED
Amsterdam
Holland

"Shiva Skunk"
Sensi Seed Bank
P.O. Box 1771
3000 BT Rotterdam
Holland

K.C. Import & Export
Alias K.C. Brains
P.O. Box 637
4200 A.P. Goriwhem
Holland

"White Widow Peacemaker"
the White Widow Master

It is illegal to import marijuana seeds into the U.S.A. and many other countries.

Lighting Appendix

This table shows how plants respond to various spectrums of light.

PRINCIPAL PHOTOCHEMICAL REACTIONS OF HIGHER PLANTS*

Photoprocess	Reaction or Response	Products	Photoreceptors	Action Spectra Peaks (mu)
		Energy Conversion		
Chlorophyll Synthesis	Reduction of Proto-chlorophyll	Chlorophyll a Chlorophyll b	Protochlorophyll	Blue: 445 Red: 640
Photosynthesis	Dissociation of H_2O into 2(H) and 1/2 O_2 and reduction of (CO_2)	Reluctant (H) Phosphorylated compounds	Chlorophylls Carotenoids	Blue: 435 Red: 675
		Regulation of Growth		
Blue Reactions	(1) Phototropism (2) Protoplasmic viscosity (3) Photoreactivation	Oxidized auxin, auxin systems and/or other components of the cell	(1) Carotenoid or flavin (2) Unknown (3) Pyridine nucleotide riboflavin, etc.	1. Near UV: 370 Blue: 445 475 2. Uncertain 3. Uncertain
Red, Far red Reactions	(1) Seed germination (2) Seedling and vegetative growth (3) Anthocyanin synthesis (4) Chloroplast responses (5) Heterotrophic growth (6) Photoperiodism (7) Chromosome response	Biochemistry completely unknown	Phytochrome	(1-6) Induc-red: 660; reversal by far-red: 710 and 730 (7) Far red induced, red reversed spectral details uncertain

* From Withrow (1959).

Courtesy, Sylvania Lighting Products, Danvers, Mass., Bulletin #0-352.

LAMPS AND PLANT RESPONSE

In studies conducted by the Department of Agriculture, plants showed different growth characteristics depending on the type of light source they were given. Here is a summary of the U.S.D.A. results:

Lamp	Plant Response
Fluorescent - Cool White (CW) and Warm White (WW).	• Green foliage expands parallel to the surface of the lamp. • Stems elongate slowly. • Multiple side shoots develop. • Flowering occurs over a long period of time.
Fluorescent - Gro Lux (GL) Plant Lights (PL)	• Deep-green foliage which expands, often larger than on plants grown under CW or WW. • Stem elongates very slowly, extra thick stems develop. • Multiple side shoots develop. • Flowering occurs late, flower stalks do not elongate.
Fluorescent - Gro Lux-WS (GL-WS), Vita-lite (VITA), Agro-lite (AGRO) and Wide Spectrum lamps.	• Light-green foliage which tends to ascend toward the lamp. • Stems elongate rapidly, distances between the leaves. • Suppresses development of multiple side shoots. • Flowering occurs soon, flower stalks elongated, plants mature and age rapidly.
High Intensity Discharge- Deluxe Mercury (HG) or Metal halide (MH).	• Similar to CW & WW fluorescent lamps compared on equal energy. • Green foliage which expands. • Stems elongate slowly. • Multiple side shoots develop. • Flowering occurs over a long period of time.
High Intensity Discharge- High pressure sodium (HPS).	• Similar to Gro Lux and other color improved fluorescent compared on equal energy. • Deep-green foliage which expands, often larger than on plants grown under H and MH. • Stems elongate very slowly, extra thick stems develop. • Multiple side shoots develop. • Flowering occurs late, flower stalks do not elongate.
High Intensity Discharge- Low Pressure Sodium (LPS)	• Extra deep-green foliage, bigger and thicker than on plants grown under other light sources. • Stem elongation is slowed, very thick stems develop. • Multiple side shoots develop even on secondary shoots. • Flowering occurs, flower stalks do not elongate. Exceptions: Saintpaulias, lettuce, and Impatiens must have supplemental sunlight or incandescent to insure development of chlorophyll and reduction of stem elongation.
Incandescent (INC) and Incandescent-Mercury (INC-HG)	• Paling of foliage, thinner and longer than on plants grown under light sources. • Stem elongation is excessive, eventually become spindly and easily breaks. • Side shoot development is suppressed, plants expand only in height. • Flowering occurs rapidly, the plants mature and senescence takes place. Exceptions: Rosette and thick-leaved plants such as Sansevieria may maintain themselves for many months. The new leaves which eventually develop will elongate and will not have the typical characteristics of the species.

From: U.S. Department of Agriculture Home and Garden Bulletin #220, "Indoor Gardening," p. 16-17.

VISUAL COLOR APPEARANCE

The U.S. Department of Agriculture investigated various types of artificial lighting in regards to color rendition and characteristics of each lamp. Here are the results of the study.

Lamp Fluorescent	Abbreviation	General Appearance on a Neutral Wall or Surface	Complexion (the actual appearance of skin)	Atmosphere (the effect or general feeling of room)	Flower Color Under Light Colors Improved or Strengthened	Greyed (undesirable)
Cool White[1]	CW	White	Pale Pink	Neutral to cool	Blue, Yellow, Orange	Red
Warm White	WW	Yellowish	Sallow	warm	Yellow, Orange	Blue, Green, Red
Gro Lux, Plant Light	GRO	Purplish White	Reddish	warm	Blue, Red	Green, Yellow
Gro Lux-WS	GRO-WS	Light Pink-White	Pink	warm	Blue, Yellow, Red	Green
Agro-lite	AGRO	White	Pink	warm	Blue, Yellow, Red	Green
Vita-lite	VITA	Bluish White	Pink	warm	Blue, Yellow, Red	Green
Discharge						
Mercury (all types)	HG	Purplish White	Ruddy	cool	Blue, Green, Yellow	Red
Metal Halide	MH	Pale Greenish White	Greyed	cool green	Blue, Green, Yellow	Red
High-Pressure Sodium	HPS	Yellowish	Yellowish	warm	Green, Yellow, Orange	Blue, Red
Low-Pressure Sodium	LPS	Orange-Yellow	Greyed	warm	Yellow	All Except Yellow
Incandescent	INC	Yellowish White	Ruddy	warm	Yellow, Orange, Red	Blue
Incandescent-Mercury	INC-HG	Yellowish White	Ruddy	warm	Yellow, Orange, Red	Blue

[1] Deluxe Cool White or Deluxe Warm White will give better color rendition than Standard Cool White or Warm White.

From: U.S. Department of Agriculture Home and Garden Bulletin, #220, "Indoor Gardening," p. 12-13.

Since plants respond to certain spectrums better than others, the quantity of light is only one factor. The other is the quality of light. In this chart cool white fluorescents are given as the standard. Each tube is rated for the amount of light it would require to supply the plant with an equal amount of usable energy. For instance, 88 footcandles (fc) from a metal halide would supply the plants with the equivalent usable energy of 100 fc of cool white. However, it would take 108 fc from a high pressure sodium.

APPROPRIATE FOOT-CANDLES[1] FOR EQUAL RADIANT ENERGY (VISIBLE 400-850 nm) FOR SELECTED LAMPS

Lamp		fc	fc	fc	fc
Fluorescent					
Cool White	CW	100	200	500	1000
Warm White	WW	105	210	525	1050
Gro-Lux, Plant Light	GRO	47	94	235	470
Gro-Lux-WS	GRO/WS	68	136	340	680
Agro-lite	AGRO	74	148	370	740
Vita-lite	VITA	80	160	400	800
Discharge					
Mercury (all types)	HG	108	216	540	1080
Metal Halide	MH	87	174	435	870
High-Pressure Sodium	HPS	88	176	440	880
Low-Pressure Sodium	LPS	137	274	685	1370
Incandescent	INC	35	70	175	350
Incandescent-Mercury	INC-HG	50	100	250	500
Sunlight:					
Winter		53	106	265	530
Summer		55	110	273	546

[1]The foot-candle readings given in the Plant Guide are based on Cool White fluorescent lamps. Note that when the table lists 100 fc of Cool White fluorescent, it requires 53 fc from sunlight, 105 fc from Warm White, 47 fc from Gro-Lux, 68 fc from Gro-Lux-WS to give equal energy and equal effectiveness for lighting plants. Check with a lighting engineer to find out what kind of artificial lamps are used to light the space.

From: U.S. Department of Agriculture
Home and Garden Bulletin, #220, "Indoor Gardening," p. 20.

This chart indicates how energy is used by light illumination sources.

Input power shows how much electricity is drawn.

Total lumens shows how much light the tube emits.

Visible radiation shows what percentage of the electricity is converted to light.

Nonvisible radiation shows how much was converted to heat or spectrums not visible to the eye.

Conduction and convection is the amount of energy lost in moving the electricity.

Ballasts are not 100% efficient. This shows their loss.

INPUT POWER CONVERSION OF LIGHT SOURCES

Fluorescent	Input Power Total Watt	Lamp Watt	Total Lumens per Lamp	Total Lumen per Watt	Visible Radiation Percent	Nonvisible Radiation Percent	Conduction & Convection Percent	Ballasts Loss Percent
Cool White	46	40	3,200	70	20	32	35	13
Warm White	46	40	3,250	71	20	32	35	13
Gro Lux, Plant Light	46	40	925	20	13	35	39	13
Gro Lux-WS	46	40	1,700	37	15	35	37	13
Agro-lite	46	40	1,900	41	15	35	37	13
Vita-lite	46	40	2,180	47	18	33	36	13
Discharge								
Mercury Deluxe	440	400	22,000	50	13	62	16	09
Metal Halide	460	400	34,000	75	20	54	13	13
High Pressure Sodium	470	400	47,000	100	25	47	13	15
Low-Pressure Sodium	230	180	33,000	143	25	47	13	15
Incandescent	100	100	1,740	17	07	83	10	0
Incandescent-Mercury	-	-	-	18-25	-	-	-	-

From: U.S. Department of Agriculture
Home And Garden Bulletin #220,
"Indoor Gardening," p. 21.

Each spectrum of light has a certain amount of energy. This energy is measured in microwatts. Different tubes and lamps have different spectrums of light. The amount of energy that the tube emits can be determined by multiplying the number of footcandles by the conversion factor.

CONVERSION FACTORS, FOOTCANDLES TO MICROWATTS
PER CM² (380-800 nm)

Lamp	Microwatts per Cm² per Footcandle
Cool White Fluorescent (40 watt)	3.18
White Fluorescent (40 watt)	3.00
Warm White Fluorescent (40 watt)	2.90
Daylight Fluorescent (40 watt)	3.71
Blue Fluorescent (40 watt) (Calcium Tungstate)	6.30
Green Fluorescent (40 watt)	2.14
Red Fluorescent (40 watt) (Magnesium Fluorogerminate)	16.82
Gold Fluorescent (40 watt)	2.76
Gro-Lux Fluorescent (40 watt) (Standard)	7.41
Wide Spectrum Gro-Lux Fluorescent Lamp	4.87
Incandescent (500 watt)	6.84
Mercury Vapor (400 watt) H33 CD-400	4.16
Mercury Vapor (400 watt) H33-400/DX	3.65
Metalarc (400 watt) M400	4.01
Metalarc (400 watt) M400/C	4.29
Lumalux (400 watt) LU-400	2.87

Courtesy, Sylvania Lighting Products
Danvers, Mass., Bulletin #0-352, p. 10.

COMPARISON OF THE ACTION SPECTRA OF THE SPED CURVES OF COOL
WHITE FLUORESCENT (A), INCANDESCENT LAMPS (B), PHOTOSYNTHETIC
RESPONSE (C), CHLOROPHYLL SYNTHESIS (D) AND EYE SENSITIVITY (E)

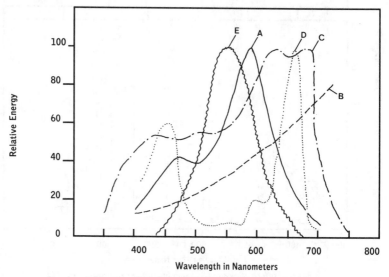

Based on information from Sylvania Lighting Products, Danvers, Mass.
Bulletin #0-352, p. 6 & 7.

SODIUM VAPOR (A) AND METAL HALIDE (B) SPECTRUMS

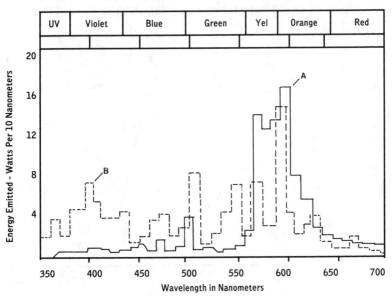

Based on information from Sylvania Lighting Products, Danvers, Mass.
Bulletin #0-352, p. 6 & 7

PHOTOSYNTHETIC RATE TO LIGHT INTENSITY AND CO₂ CONCENTRATION

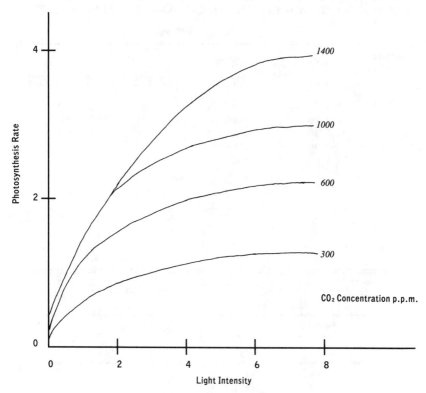

The Effect of a Range of Concentrations of CO₂ And Irradiation Values
on the Photosynthetic Rate
Courtesy, Sylvania Lighting Products, Danvers, Mass.
Bulletin #0-352, p. 5

ILLUMINATION IN FOOTCANDLES AT VARIOUS DISTANCES FROM COOL WHITE OR WARM WHITE FLUORESCENT LAMPS AND INCANDESCENTS[1]

4 Ft. Standard 40 Watt[2]

Distance from Lamp Feet	2-F40	2-F40	4-F40	6-F40
0.5	500	700	900	1000
1	260 (200)	400 (260)	600	700
2	110 (100)	180 (150)	330	450
3	60 (60)	100 (90)		
4	40	60	100	140

4 Ft. VHO 115W

	2-F48	4-F48	6-F48
1	900	1700	2000
2	400	740	1100

	INCANDESCENT Standard Lamp		INCANDESCENT PAR-38	
	40 W	60 W	75 W	150 W
1	34 (17)	67 (33)		
2	8 (7)	17 (13)		
3	4 (3)	7 (7)	375 (40)	383 (80)
4			167 (40)	216 (110)
5	(double values with		94 (50)	138 (90)
6	reflectors)		60 (40)	96 (70)

[1] Values in parentheses are footcandles one foot on either side of lamp perpendicular to distance below lamps.
[2] End views.

From: U.S. Department of Agriculture Home and Garden Bulletin #220,
"Indoor Gardening," p. 14.

Photosynthesis Appendix

Light may influence many phases of growth, however, Photosynthesis, Chlorophyll synthesis, Phototropism, Photomorphogenic red-induction and Photomorphogenic far-red-reversal, and Photoperiodism are most directly controlled by light. The action spectra of the above photoresponses are shown in Figures 1 and 2.

Photosynthesis

Life on our planet depends on the key event, photosynthesis. This is putting together, by means of light, two simple substances – carbon dioxide and water – to form carbohydrates, the basic food for all living organisms, and releasing oxygen as a byproduct. During the light period, respiration continues simultaneously and some of the oxygen is utilized in this process. At night, photosynthesis stops, but the respiratory process continues. The green pigment, chlorophyll, plays a vital role in photosynthesis.

The current understanding of this series of reactions is backed by experimental evidence which indicates that absorbed light energy causes electrons in chlorophyll to become ''active.'' In this ''active'' higher energy state the electrons move to other molecules. The chlorophyll acts not as isolated molecules but in a linked group of molecules, somewhat as a photobattery. By a series of intermediate electron ''carrier''' molecules, the electrons are used in enzyme reactions which bind hydrogen with carbon forming carbohydrates and also to link phosphate groups to form the important intermediate energy carrier molecules. This energy can be used to synthesize more complex organic compounds. The oxygen is released into the atmosphere as a by-product. In short, it is an oxidation-reduction reaction. Removal of electrons and hydrogen from water is oxidation, and the combining of hydrogen with carbon from carbon dioxide is reduction. This is accomplished in a series of very involved chemical steps, but we need only be concerned with the end result, production of carbohydrates. A number of complex sugars are produced from the simple carbohydrates first formed, and with further chemical processing by reactions of metabolism more compounds are developed, such as cellulose, fats and proteins.

Studies conducted with wheat plants, in which all wavelengths were transmitted with equal intensity, indicated that the action spectra for photosynthetic carbon fixation has a peak in the red band (675 nanometers) and another in the blue (435 nanometers). It is interesting to note that the maxima for photosynthesis practically coincide with the action spectra of chlorophyll (see Figure 1) synthesis which occurs at 650 nanometers (red) and 445 nanometers (blue).

Chlorophyll Synthesis

In higher plants, light is required for the formation of chlorophyll, which is the green coloring matter of plants produced by the chloroplasts of the cell. Plants left in darkness for a few days become yellow because the chlorophylls decompose. When exposed to light, chlorophyll is synthesized immediately and the plant begins to turn green in a matter of hours. The important spectral regions of chlorophyll synthesis are in the red (650 nm) and blue (445 nm) Figure 1. The chlorophyll in higher plants is of two forms (a) and (b) which are closely related chemically. In many green plants, quantity of chlorophyll (a) is about three times that of chlorophyll (b).

Fig. 1 Action Spectrum of: (A) Photosynthetic Response, And (B) Chlorophyll Synthesis

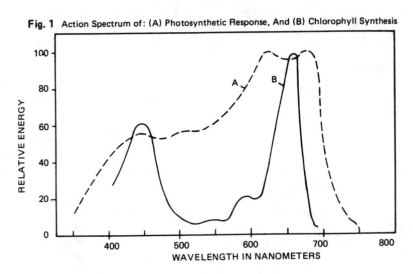

Phototropism

The specific movement of a plant part to illumination is termed phototropism. The term, Positive Tropism, is used to indicate that the plant bends toward the light source, while Negative Tropism, indicates that the growth is away from the light source.

The sunflower is so named because, in the growing plant the heads are turned toward the east in the morning and toward the west in the evening, following the course of the sun.

Phototropic responses are not equal in all parts of the visible spectrum. Some researchers have found that the most effective wavelengths ranged from 400 to 480 nanometers, which are the violet and blue regions of the spectrum (Figure 2). No phototropic effect is produced by the red end of the spectrum. For this reason, quantitative determinations of auxins (natural hormones) are made in the red light.

In the green region, the phototropic effect is very slight. Phototropism may be manifested under very low intensities. It should be recalled that the photochemical effect of light on plants equals the product of time and intensity.

Fig. 2 Action Spectrum Of: (A) Phototropic Response (B) Photopic Vision (Eye Sensitivity Curve), (C) Photomorphogenic Induction (Pr), (D) Photomorphogenic Reversal (Pfr)

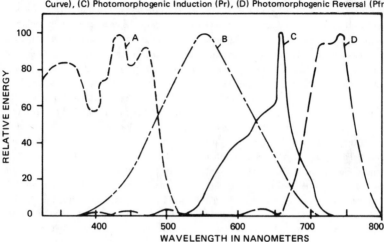

Photomorphogenesis

This photoresponse is initiated largely by the phytochrome reaction and governs the development and differentiation of growth responses. Many research studies have been conducted but it is only in the last few years that the phytochrome molecule has been isolated. This molecule is a protein, blue in color, that acts as an enzyme, and occurs in two reversible forms. In one form, known as Pr or P660, the phytochrome has the absorption characteristic shown in Figure 2, with a peak at 660 nanometers. Radiation of this wavelength is absorbed by the Pr which then changes into the second form Pfr or P735. The phytochrome can no longer absorb red radiation but has absorption responses as shown in Figure 2 with a peak at 735 nanometers in the far-red region. The effect of absorbing this type of radiation is to restore the phytochrome to the Pr form. This change also takes place in darkness, but at a slower rate. This reversible reaction can be represented as folllows:

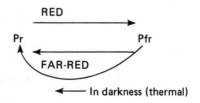

The Pfr form is regarded as the active form in a number of physiological processes, and the Pr the inactive form of phytochrome. The rate of change in darkness is dependent on temperature. Among the responses now known to be dependent on phytochrome are photoperiodism, stem elongation, seed germination and the synthesis of anthocyanin.

The phytochrome reaction responds to comparatively low levels of radiant energy, but a second reaction has been discovered which is also involved in photomorphogenesis but which depends on high energy levels maintained for comparatively long periods of time. This reaction has become known as the ''High-Energy Reaction'' although the term ''Prolonged Light Reaction (PLR)'' is preferred since duration is of prime importance. The theory is far from well established but the action spectrum has been determined (Figure 3) and shows maxima in the blue and far-red regions of the spectrum. Unlike the common phytochrome reaction, the prolonged light reaction is not reversible. A good illustration of a plant reaction which appears to depend on both prolonged light reaction and on the presence of phytochrome, is the formation of anthocyanin which is produced as a result of a prolonged light reaction with the maximum response at 470 nanometers, but the process could only be completed in the presence of Pfr. A subsequent exposure to far-red radiation converts the Pfr and Pr and inhibits the synthesis of anthocyanin, but this can be re-promoted by a further exposure to red light (pr).

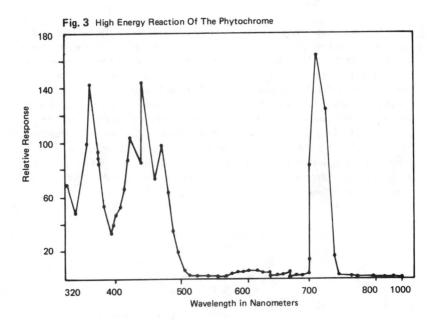

Fig. 3 High Energy Reaction Of The Phytochrome

Photoperiodism

It was learned by two United States Department of Agriculture scientists, W.W. Garner and A.A. Allard, in about 1920 that there is a relationship between the length of the dark period and the light period, which affects all plants. This relationship, they noted, prevented Maryland Mammoth tobacco from flowering unless the day was short and the night was long. This response was called photoperiodism, and soon plants came to be classified as long-day plants if they needed a long day to flower, and short-day plants if they needed a short day to flower. Later developments, however, showed that the critical factor was the length of the dark period, not the light period.

It was found that using the cocklebur as a sensitive short-day plant, only a minute's exposure to a bright light in the middle of the dark period was necessary to prevent blooming, whereas interrupting the light period with brief darkness had no effect.

Researchers have found that red light (peak 660 nm) is the vital part of the visible spectrum influencing photoperiodic responses.

A theory of the photoperiod action based on a hypothetical flowering hormone ''florigen'' may be summarized as follows: Florigen is subject to destruction by light. A certain critical concentration of this substance is necessary for induction of flowering, but a large quantity prevents blooming. Short-day plants require a long, dark period to accumulate sufficient quantities of the hormone to induce blooming. The theory stipulates that the flowering hormone in long-day plants is protected from photosensitized destruction. Some plant scientists are of the opinion that the substance which finally controls flowering may be at the end of a chain of reactions, and that light reaction is possibly only the first link in the chain.

Measurement of Light Energy

Since radiant energy for plant growth is not the same as visual illumination for the human eye, the footcandle is unsuitable as a unit of measurement of radiant energy for plant responses. The footcandle is based upon the spectral sensitivity of the human eye; it is wavelength selective with the maximum response from 550 to 560, as shown in Figure 4. However, the footcandle meter can be a very useful tool in establishing intensity levels and uniform light distribution over plants. For the range of 300 nm to 700 nm, the footcandle measurement can be converted to meaningful absolute energy units for any conventional light source. See table entitled 'Conversion Factors Footcandles to Microwatts per CM^2 which gives the conversion factors for several light sources.

Instruments for measuring light energy in absolute units or quantum units such as microwatts per square centimeter are essential for scientific work with horticultural lighting. These instruments include such devices as the thermopile, bolometers, spectroradiometers and quantum sensors. These instruments have a response within a wide energy range and over a broad wavelength band. The spectroradiometers range from portable plant growth photometers, which measure energy in absolute units for the three major spectral response regions previously mentioned (400 to 500, 600 to 700, and 700 to 800), to stationary laboratory types which measure radiant energy from the ultraviolet through the infrared spectral regions.

EYE SENSITIVITY CURVE

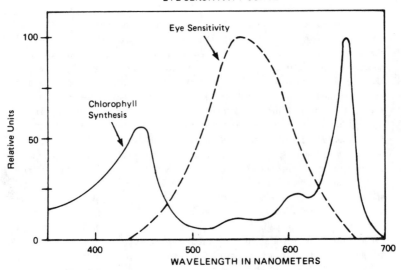

Fig. 4   Spectral Activity Of The Chlorophyll Synthesis Process. Visual Sensitivity Curve is
Shown For Comparison.

For practical considerations, it is usually more convenient to express light intensity
for commercial horticultural lighting in terms of lamp watts per square foot of growing
area – with the light source at a given distance from the plants. This enables the plants-
man to determine the number of lamps needed for a particular area and the power used.

The formula for calcuating the number of lamps for an installation is:

Number of lamps =

$$\frac{\text{Growing area X lamp watts/ft}^2 \text{ required}}{\text{Individual lamp watts}}$$

Other advantages of using lamp watts per square foot include:

1. Greater accuracy than that of a footcandle reading for comparing lamps of different spectral energy distribution curves.
2. Simplified calculations in the cost per square foot for installation and operation
   of a lighting system.

Excerpted from Horticultural Light Sources, Engineering bulletin 0-352
Christos C. Mpelkas,
Plant Physiologist,
Lighting Products Group
GTE Sylvania
Danvers, Massachusetts

Bibliography

1. All About Fertilizers, Soils and Water. 1979. 112 pp. Ortho Books Editorial Staff. Ortho Books, Chevron Chemical Company, San Francisco, California.
2. Aphids in the Home Garden and Landscape. July, 1979. 7 pp. Division of Agricultural Sciences, University of California, Berkeley, California. Leaflet #21032.
3. Aphids on Leafy Vegetables. Revised 1977. 18 pp. USDA. Washington, D.C., Stock #001-000-03651-3.
4. Applying Nutrients and Other Chemicals to Trickle Irrigated Crops. April, 1981. 14 pp. Division of Agricultural Sciences, University of California, Berkeley, California. Leaflet #1893.
5. Bickford, Elwood D., and Dunn, Stuart. 1972. Lighting for Plant Growth. 221 pp. Kent State University Press.
6. Branch, Diana S., Editor. 1978. Tools for Homesteaders, Gardeners, and Small-Scale Farmers. 512 pp. Rodale Press, Inc., Emmaus, Pennsylvania.
7. Bridwell, Raymond. 1974. Hydroponic Gardening. 224 pp. Woodbridge Press Publishing Company, Santa Barbara, California.
8. California Agriculture, *continuing.* Published by University of California Division of Agriculture and Natural Resources, Berkeley, California.
9. Campbell, Stu. 1975. Let it Rot! The Home Gardener's Guide to Composting. 152 pp. Garden Way Publishing, Charlotte, Vermont.
10. Carr, Anna. 1979. Rodale's Color Handbook of Garden Insects. 241 pp. Rodale Press, Inc., Emmaus, Pennsylvania.
11. Cervantes, Jorge. 1974. Indoor Marijuana Horticulture. 132 pp. Interport, USA, Inc., Portland, Oregon.
12. Clarke, Robert Connell. 1981. Marijuana Botany. 197 pp. And/Or Press, Berkeley, California.
13. Container Planting. 1961. 48 pp. Countryside Books, Barrington, Illinois.
14. Drip Irrigation for the Home Garden and Landscape. June, 1978. 12 pp. Division of Agricultural Sciences, University of California, Berkeley, California. Leaflet #21025.
15. Ecology of Compost: A Public Involvement Project. March, 1981. 10 pp. Division of Agricultural Sciences, University of California, Berkeley, California. Leaflet #21200.
16. Florists' Review, *continuing.* Published by Florists' Publishing Company, Chicago, Illinois.
17. Frank, Mel, and Rosenthal, Ed. 1978. Marijuana Grower's Guide, Deluxe Edition. 330 pp. And/Or Press, Berkeley, California.

18. Frazier, Jack. 1974. The Marijuana Farmers: Hemp Cults and Cultures. 133 pp. Solar Age Press, New Orleans, Louisiana.
19. Gardening: A House & Garden Guide. 1979. 152 pp. Conde Nast Publications, Inc., New York, New York.
20. Gardening for Food and Fun. 1977. 392 pp. USDA. Washington, D.C., Stock #001-000-03679-3.
21. The Gardener's Helper. 1982. 116 pp. Editors of Organic Gardening Magazine. Rodale Press, Inc., Emmaus, Pennsylvania.
22. Getting the Bugs out of Organic Gardening. 1973. 115 pp. Editors of Organic Gardening and Farming. Rodale Press, Inc., Emmaus, Pennsylvania.
23. Goleuke, Clarence G. 1972. Composting: A Study of the Process and Its Principles. 110 pp. Rodale Press, Inc., Emmaus, Pennsylvania.
24. Growing Plants Without Soil for Experimental Use. December, 1972. 17 pp. USDA, Washington, D.C., Stock #0-474-858.
25. Gypsum and Other Chemical Amendments for Soil Improvement. March, 1980. 7 pp. Division of Agricultural Sciences, University of California, Berkeley, California. Leaflet #2149.
26. Halpin, Anne M., Editor, 1982. The Organic Gardener's Complete Guide to Vegetables and Fruits. 510 pp. Rodale Press, Inc., Emmaus, Pennsylvania.
27. Handbook on Propagation. (Special Printing Vol. 13, No. 2). 1965. 80 pp. The Brooklyn Botanic Garden, Brooklyn, New York.
28. Hessayon, D.G. 1973. Be Your Own House Plant Expert. 34 pp. Pan Britannica Industries, Ltd., Waltham Cross, Herts, England.
29. How to Multiply Your Plants. 1976. 31 pp. The John Henry Company, Lansing, Michigan.
30. Hoye, David. 1973. Cannabis Alchemy. 109 pp. Twentieth Century Alchemist Series/And/Or Press, Berkeley, California.
31. Indoor Gardens with Controlled Lighting. May, 1971. 22 pp. USDA, Washington, D.C., Stock #0-422-051.
32. Insects and Diseases of Vegetables in the Home Garden. March, 1975. 50 pp. USDA, Washington, D.C., Stock #001-000-03381-6.
33. Irving, Don. 1978. Guide to Growing Marijuana in the British Isles. 48 pp. Hassle Free Press, BCM Box 311, London, England.
34. Johnsen, Jan. 1979. Gardening Without Soil. 83 pp. J.B. Lippincott, New York, New York.
35. Jones, Lem. 1977. Home Hydroponics and How to Do It. 142 pp. Distributed by Crown Publishers, New York, New York.
36. Jordan, William H., Jr. 1977. Windowsill Ecology: Controlling Indoor Plant Pests With Beneficial Insects. 229 pp. Rodale Press, Inc., Emmaus, Pennsylvania.
37. Kayo. 1982. The Sinsemilla Technique. 134 pp. Last Gasp of San Francisco, California.
38. Koster, Oliver M. 1979. Introduction to Hydroponic Gardening: Utilizing the Wick System. 78 pp. Recmar Corporation, Tustin, California.
39. Langer, Richard W. 1975. Grow It Indoors. 400 pp. Saturday Review Press/E.P.Dutton & Co., Inc., New York, New York.

40. Mealybugs on House Plants and in the Home Landscape. December, 1980. 3 pp. Division of Agricultural Sciences, University of California, Berkeley, California. Leaflet #21197.
41. Managing Clay Soils in the Home Garden. September, 1976. 2 pp. Division of Agricultural Sciences, University of California, Berkeley, California. Leaflet #2634.
42. Merlin, Mark David. 1973. Man and Marijuana: Some Aspects of their Ancient Relationship. 120 pp. A.S. Barnes and Company, Inc., Cranbury, New Jersey.
43. Mites in the Home Garden and Landscape. January, 1979. 7 pp. Division of Agricultural Sciences, University of California, Berkeley, California. Leaflet #21048.
44. The Mother Earth News, *continuing*. Published by Mother Earth News, Inc., Hendersonville, North Carolina.
45. The New Farm, *continuing*. Published by Regenerative Agriculture Association, Emmaus, Pennsylvania.
46. Nicholls, Richard. 1975. The Plant Doctor. 108 pp. Running Press, Philadelphia, Pennsylvania.
47. Olkowski, Helga. 1971. Common Sense Pest Control. 52 pp. Consumers Cooperative of Berkeley, Inc., Richmond, California.
48. Optimiser System. August, 1982. Published by General Electric. Pamphlet #203-21324.
49. Organic Gardening, continuing. Published by Rodale Press, Inc., Emmaus, Pennsylvania.
50. The Penguin Dictionary of Botany. 1984. 390 pp. Penguin Books, New York, New York.
51. Pocket Guide to Pest Management. 1980. 106 pp. Naval Air Stations in Jacksonville, Florida, and Alameda, California. Stock #008-045-00022-4.
52. Resh, Howard M., 1978. Hydroponic Food Production. 287 pp. Woodbridge Press Publishing Company, Santa Barbara, California.
53. Rodale, J.I. 1961. How to Grow Vegetables & Fruits by the Organic Method. 926 pp. Rodale Press, Inc., Emmaus, Pennsylvania.
54. Riotte, Louise. 1975. Carrots Love Tomatoes. 225 pp. Garden Way Publishing, Charlotte, Vermont.
55. Riotte, Louise. 1977. Success with Small Food Gardens, Using Special Intensive Methods. 189 pp. Garden Way Associates/Essex Publishing Company, Charlotte, Vermont.
56. Sanders, Robert E., Editor. 1976. A to Z Hints for the Vegetable Gardener. 119 pp. Men's Garden Clubs of America, Des Moines, Iowa.
57. Sinsemilla Tips: Domestic Grower's Journal, *continuing*. Published by New Moon Publishing, Corvallis, Oregon.
58. Solomon, Steve. 1984. Raising Transplants at Home. 22 pp. Territorial Seed Company, Lorane, Oregon.
59. Spider Mite Pests of Cotton. May, 1976. 7 pp. Division of Agricultural Sciences, University of California, Berkeley, California. Leaflet #2888.
60. Starks, Michael. 1977. Marijuana Potency. 174 pp. And/Or Press, Berkeley, California.

61. Stevens, Murphy. 1975. How to Grow Marijuana Indoors Under Lights. 75 pp. Sun Magic Publishing Company, Seattle, Washington.
62. Taylor, James D., 1983. Grow More Nutritious Vegetables Without Soil. 298 pp. ParkSide Press Publishing Company, Santa Ana, California.
63. 300 of the Most Asked Questions About Organic Gardening. 1972. 186 pp. Editors of Organic Gardening Magazine. Rodale Press, Inc., Emmaus, Pennsylvania, and Bantam Books, New York, New York.
64. Using Household Waste Water on Plants. April, 1977. 2 pp. Division of Agricultural Sciences, University of California, Berkeley, California. Leaflet #2968.
65. Western Garden Book. 1977. 447 pp. Editors of Sunset Magazine. Lane Publishing Company, Menlo Park, California.
66. Yepsen, Roger B., Jr., Editor. 1976. Organic Plant Protection, 688 pp. Rodale Press, Inc., Emmaus, Pennsylvania.

Index

Back cover

Closet Cultivator emphasizes small spaces, simplicity and high yields. The book features a full color, close-up look at: Buds, Males & Females, Gardens, Problems, Pests, Systems, and of course More Buds. The step-by-step directions cover the newest techniques. It's perfect for every cannabis enthusiast.
$16.95

"Ed, the famous **Ask Ed** ... is an entire set of encyclopedias when it comes to growing pot. If knowledge is power, Ed Rosenthal is General Electric."
—Dr. A. Sumach, *Cannabis Culture*

ALSO AVAILABLE AT YOUR LOCAL BOOKSTORE

Marihuana Reconsidered

by Dr. Lester Grinspoon, M.D.

Back in print! First published by Harvard University Press in 1971, this is still the most comprehensive assessment of marihuana and its place in society. Noted psychiatrist, Dr. Lester Grinspoon pulverizes the arguments that keep marihuana illegal. Updated with a new introduction by the author who still believes that the most dangerous thing about smoking and marihuana is getting caught.

$19.95

Why Marijuana Should Be Legal

By Ed Rosenthal and Steve Kubby

This concise and pointed argument should be on every smoker's bookshelf. Logical, no-nonsense discussions of the costs, benefits, and implications of the legalization of marijuana will help convince anyone it's the way to go.

$9.95

Marijuana Medical Handbook:
A Guide to Therapeutic Use

by Ed Rosenthal, Dale Gieringer, and Tod Mikuriya, M.D.

This guide offers information on how to use and procure marijuana for medicine. It provides the most up-to-date, scientific methods for smoking and eating this medicinal herb. A concise cultivation section by expert Ed Rosenthal explains plant basics and shows an easy way to set up a personal use garden.

$16.95

www.quicktrading.com

online home of Ask Ed™

Grow Tips

Politics

Links to the best cannabis sites

Buds

Marijuana Question:
Come online and Ask Ed